Dependent
Origination
in Plain English

DEPENDENT ORIGINATION
IN PLAIN ENGLISH

*Bhante Gunaratana
and Veronique Ziegler*

Wisdom Publications
132 Perry Street
New York, NY 10014 USA
wisdomexperience.org

Library of Congress Cataloging-in-Publication Data
Names: Gunaratana, Henepola, 1927– author. | Ziegler, Veronique, author.
Title: Dependent origination in plain English /
    Bhante Gunaratana and Veronique Ziegler.
Description: First edition. | New York: Wisdom Publications, 2024. |
    Includes bibliographical references and index.
Identifiers: LCCN 2023045690 (print) | LCCN 2023045691 (ebook) |
    ISBN 9781614298984 (paperback) | ISBN 9781614299141 (ebook)
Subjects: LCSH: Pratītyasamutpāda. | Theravāda Buddhism—Doctrines.
Classification: LCC BQ4240 .G86 2024 (print) | LCC BQ4240 (ebook) |
    DDC 294.3/42041—dc23/eng/20231025
LC record available at https://lccn.loc.gov/2023045690
LC ebook record available at https://lccn.loc.gov/2023045691

ISBN 978-1-61429-898-4   ebook ISBN 978-1-61429-914-1

28 27 26 25 24
5 4 3 2 1

Cover design by Phil Pascuzzo. Interior design by Gopa & Ted2, Inc.

Printed on acid-free paper that meets the guidelines for permanence
and durability of the Production Guidelines for Book Longevity
of the Council on Library Resources.

Printed in Canada.

Please visit fscus.org.

 *Contents*

Preface   vii

A Note on Language   ix

Introduction   1

1. Ignorance   7

2. Sankharas   45

3. Consciousness   69

4. Mentality and Materiality   77

5. The Sixfold Base   81

6. The Nutriment of Contact   85

7. Feeling   89

8. Craving   101

9. Clinging   115

10. Becoming   121

11. Birth   123

12. Death and the Arising of This Entire Mass of Suffering   129

Reflecting on Impermanence   133

Reversing the Chain   135

Acknowledgments   141

Abbreviations   143

Notes   145

Bibliography   147

Index   149

About the Authors   155

Preface

THE THEORY of dependent origination describes the causes and conditions involved in anything that occurs in our lives; by studying it, we can discover a roadmap to the ultimate liberation from suffering. The physical and mental states that we experience at a particular time depend on certain causes and conditions that we experience daily. Our mental states are generally afflicted by positive or negative moods, and our bodies similarly experience pleasure or pain. To overcome suffering we must understand it and have a deep grasp of its nature and cause. There are multiple books and articles on dependent origination, but this is not just another book. It is a very practical, down-to-earth guide written in plain English so that anyone—scholar or non-scholar—can understand the message.

Dependent origination explains the mechanism that keeps us in a state of suffering and presents a clear and straightforward solution to attain total freedom from all suffering. We start with explaining the formula and laying out the foundation for the twelve steps involved with the theory before going through the details of each step in the following chapters. Throughout the book we present the details and roadmap relevant to gain direct insight into dependent origination and apply it in our lives.

In this book we don't discuss dependent origination in terms of past, present, and future lives but rather expound on the causes and conditions that happen here and now in our present existence. Whatever we are experiencing, our feelings and emotions are all happening here and now, and so it would not be helpful to dwell in the past or project into the future to find inner peace and contentment. The solution is in the present.

This is a collection of my talks on this topic given over a period of several years. One of the students attending this series of lectures, Veronique Ziegler, transcribed them all and painstakingly polished their content. We then discussed and revised the material several times to turn it into a book. It is our wish that this book helps you gain insight into dependent origination, inspires you to apply it in your life, and ultimately gives you the tools to attain liberation.

A Note on Language

THIS BOOK utilizes words from the Pali canon, ancient texts ascribed to the Buddha, written down from an oral tradition that for hundreds of years after his passing was the only method of preserving his words. These verses are like a road map or a driver's manual to the experience of freedom.

Pali is a technical language for Buddhist meditation training, conveying some concepts in ways that English cannot. While words that might be new to the reader or those that play a significant methodological role will appear in italics at their first use, words in popular usage will be left as is, such as *Buddha*, here denoting the enlightened being born as Siddhattha Gotama (or, in Sanskrit, Siddhartha Gautama); *Dhamma*, the teachings of that buddha or the natural law of all things, sometimes meaning "phenomena"; and *Sangha*, in this case referring to the community of enlightened Buddhist monastics. Other concepts such as *bhikkhu*, the term for monk, and *sutta*, a teaching discourse, will be used interchangeably with their English counterparts as appropriate.

Regarding citations, all quotations from the classical texts are translated by the author unless otherwise noted. Diacritics have been omitted from these for ease of reading. In many other cases we use translations by Bhikkhu Bodhi; for those, we have included diacritics out of respect and gratitude for his work. Although the translated passages contained in this book might seem repetitive, please remember that this stylistic aspect of the texts helped monks with memorization so as to keep the teachings alive during the hundreds of years before writing became available, and importantly, it will also remind contemporary readers to place their attention precisely in very specific ways, over and over again, a process that is necessary to achieve the goal of meditation. Practicing with the Pali in this way will make juicy and rich that which might otherwise seem dry or monotonous. It is hoped that the reader will encounter great benefit from contemplation according to these timeless instructions.

Introduction

SUFFERING DOES NOT arise independently. It arises based on certain conditions, and when those conditions are eliminated, it ceases. This, in short, is the teaching of dependent origination, and it leads to the complete elimination of ignorance, the cause of suffering. As long as ignorance is there, suffering is there. As long as greed, hatred, and delusion are there, suffering is there. If you want to get rid of your suffering, remove greed, hatred, and delusion from your mind.

The Buddha's teachings guide us to study ourselves in the minutest detail to understand accurately what is going on within us. Studying dependent origination leads us to self-exploration, to observing within our own body and mind the dependent arising and dependent ceasing of our psychosomatic responses to our experiences in the world. It is very applicable to our daily lives, but what exactly does the term *dependent* mean? When asked, for instance, if it is going to rain today, we would answer, "It depends." But universal causation states that everything has a cause and an effect produced by that cause, and therefore the arising of one thing (the effect) depends upon the arising of another thing (the cause). And conversely if the cause does not arise, the effect also cannot arise.

According to Buddhist scriptures, while sitting under the Bodhi tree on the night of his enlightenment, the Buddha investigated the cause of suffering and saw how suffering arises and the way leading to its complete cessation. In the first watch of the night, he saw the sequences of causes and conditions leading to suffering, in the second watch the causes and conditions leading to the cessation of suffering, and in the third watch the ascending and descending order of the causes and conditions.

The general belief during the Buddha's lifetime, just as today, was that suffering just happened by accident or that it was created by oneself, others, or a combination of these. But dependent origination demonstrates that everything is conditioned, that nothing comes into existence independently, without causes and conditions. *Conditioned* means that the existence of whatever is observed, felt, experienced, and inferred depends upon another thing and that everything is interdependent and interconnected. The very word *conditioned* implies the dependent origination formula, which presents the causes and conditions leading from the root cause of suffering to its manifestation in twelve steps, connected by eleven links.

However, merely memorizing these twelve steps is neither knowing nor understanding dependent origination. It is a deep, elaborate, and comprehensive teaching that leads us to a profound understanding of ourselves and ultimately a state of absolute inner peace and serenity. In the broadest sense it applies to anything in the universe, for everything exists depending on something else: the formation of the earth is due to the formation of clumps of rocks from swirling gas and dust brought together by the force of gravity. No system in the universe can exist by itself but rather in dependence on other systems and natural phenomena that themselves occur based on natural causes and conditions. Dependent origination is a universal law that applies to nature as a whole, but in this book we only consider a segment of this all-inclusive topic, focusing on observing it in our mind-body complex according to the Buddha's teachings as presented in the Buddhist suttas.

The Pali word for suffering, *dukkha*, means bearing with difficulty. Whatever we bear continuously with difficulty and without any respite is suffering. In his first sermon, *The Discourse on Turning the Wheel of Dhamma*, and in his teachings on dependent origination, the Buddha called the lump sum of the five aggregates (the basic constituents of our mind-body complex) a mountain of suffering. Without the aggregates there could be no suffering, for it can only be experienced through them.

And as one cannot escape the aggregates, the suffering they bring about is inevitable. The goal of our spiritual practice is to be free from the burden of this mountain of suffering. It is a daily endeavor.

The development of wisdom and insight is sustained by right living, the guidelines of which are laid out in the noble eightfold path. The noble eightfold path consists of right view, intention, speech, action, livelihood, effort, mindfulness, and concentration. The Buddha explains that this is the middle way between extreme asceticism and hedonism, a middle way that when followed with diligence gives vision and knowledge and leads to peace and enlightenment. Sustained effort is required to chip away at the mountain of suffering little by little every day. You must carry out the bulk of the work by developing your own practice.

THE DEPENDENT ORIGINATION FORMULA AND ITS TWELVE STEPS

The formula of dependent origination presents a causal relationship of origination and is presented following a forward order, a backward order, and a combination of both forward and backward orders.

In the forward order, the formula is "This being, this is; from the arising of this, this arises." Note that the formula states *this* and not *that*, because *this* is what is happening now, in this present moment. It refers to what is happening at this very instant in our own body and mind. Understanding the distinction between *this* and *that* in the formula is of the utmost importance. *This* indicates a thing or a situation that is close, in the present moment, while *that* points to something that is farther away or out there in some future time. *This* is all right here and right now.

We can observe the dependent origination formula at any time within ourselves. Take the example of anger. When we are angry, how do we feel? We get all hot and bothered, don't we? It happens right now, doesn't it? It is not something out there in a different time and place, where you get angry one day and then wake up the next morning agitated. Our bodies respond to anger right away: when anger rises, so does our blood pressure. From the arising of this, this arises.

In the reverse order, the formula is "This not being, this is not; from the ceasing of this, this ceases." This order presents the sequence leading to the ultimate destruction of ignorance and as a result the total liberation from suffering.

While sitting under the Bodhi tree on the night of his enlightenment, the Buddha realized the formula of dependent origination. He saw himself being reborn in samsara, the endless cycle of birth and death, life after life, and he saw other beings also being reborn again and again. As he investigated the cause of this in the minutest details during the first watch of the night, he discerned the twelve steps of dependent origination in the forward order:

1. Dependent on ignorance, volitional formations arise.
2. Dependent on volitional formations, consciousness arises.
3. Dependent on consciousness, mentality and materiality arise.
4. Dependent on mentality and materiality, the sixfold base arises.
5. Dependent on the sixfold base, contact arises.
6. Dependent on contact, feeling arises.
7. Dependent on feeling, craving arises.
8. Dependent on craving, clinging arises.
9. Dependent on clinging, becoming arises.
10. Dependent on becoming, birth arises.
11. Dependent on birth, aging, death, sorrow, lamentation, pain, grief, and despair arise.
12. Thus, there is the arising of this whole mass of suffering.[1]

In the second watch of the night, the Buddha discerned dependent origination in the reverse order:

1. Through the entire cessation of this ignorance, volitional formations cease.
2. Through the cessation of volitional formations, consciousness ceases.
3. Through the cessation of consciousness, mentality and materiality cease.
4. Through the cessation of mentality and materiality, the sixfold base ceases.
5. Through the cessation of the sixfold base, contact ceases.
6. Through the cessation of contact, feeling ceases.
7. Through the cessation of feeling, craving ceases.
8. Through the cessation of craving, clinging ceases.
9. Through the cessation of clinging, becoming ceases.
10. Through the cessation of becoming, birth ceases.
11. Through the cessation of birth, aging, death, sorrow, lamentation, pain, grief, and despair cease.
12. Thus, there is the cessation of this whole mass of suffering.[2]

In the following chapters we will explain how each of these twelve factors of dependent origination come to be and describe a method leading to the cessation of each one, culminating in the complete liberation from suffering.

As the sun rose in the early morning, the light chasing away darkness, the Buddha vanquished the ten armies of all attachments, clinging, cravings, and unwholesome traits that keep one bound to the endless cycle of rebirth, pain, sorrow, lamentations, and death. These are called the army of Mara, who represents "the personification of the forces antagonistic to enlightenment": (1) desire for sensual pleasures; (2) discontent; (3) hunger and thirst; (4) craving; (5) dullness and drowsiness; (6) cowardice; (7) doubt; (8) denigration and pride; (9) gain, praise, honor, and wrongly attained fame; and (10) exalting oneself and looking down upon others.[3] The first army, desire, exists because of ignorance, which is the first factor of dependent origination. When the Buddha saw dependent origination, then, he saw how to eliminate desire through eliminating ignorance. Once desire is destroyed so is ignorance, along with all the armies of Mara.

In the third watch of the night, the Buddha combined the forward and reverse orders. He observed a commonality in all twelve steps of dependent origination: rising and falling, or arising and vanishing. Craving arises and vanishes, volitional formations arise and vanish, and likewise for all phenomena in the twelve steps of dependent origination. He observed that whatever arises is subject to falling. He saw the arising and passing away of sensual pleasures and observed even the desire for sensual pleasures slowly fading away.

One should examine all this for oneself. Just watch what happens to desire. Watch it arising and slowly fading away. Then, the second obstacle comes: discontent and dissatisfaction with the practice. This comes and slowly fades away, too. Hunger and thirst come and fade away. And then cravings arise and fade away, first for sense pleasures, which are pleasures enjoyed through the eyes, ears, nose, tongue, body, and mind. When this vanishes, this vanishes. Not one single aspect of this dependent origination stays the same. So, in short, what the Buddha saw is rising and falling—that is, impermanence.

CHAPTER 1

Ignorance

WHAT IS IGNORANCE?

A S YOU READ this chapter, be careful to do so impartially and mindfully, without getting carried away by extreme emotions. What we are going to tell you may be disagreeable to some people. Our purpose, however, is not to say things to please people but to mention the truth that the Buddha has very clearly stated in his discourses. To be educated academically, have several university degrees, and be well versed in a great number of subjects is a kind of knowledge. But knowledge and wisdom are not the same. In Buddhism ignorance is the lack of wisdom (not simply intellectual but direct and experiential) regarding dependent origination, the noble eightfold path, and the four noble truths of suffering, the origin of suffering, the cessation of suffering, and the way leading to the cessation of suffering. We therefore caution readers not to misinterpret the word *ignorance*.

Many educated brahmins came to question the Buddha, and although they had a vast knowledge of scriptures and etymologies, they did not understand the four noble truths. Without this wisdom, academic knowledge does not lead to liberation. Knowing the four noble truths is one thing. Realizing them is another. Knowing them as a theory, a logical sequence that can be learned or memorized, is not enough. One must realize the four noble truths exactly as taught by the Buddha through one's own experience and direct knowledge. Those who have realized them have overcome ignorance.

At the time of the Buddha there was a learned and respected elder monk named Pothila, who learned this lesson for himself. He was eloquent, explained the Dhamma clearly, and had a great many students who regularly attended his lectures. One day he went to see the Buddha, but instead of addressing him by his monastic name, the Buddha called him "empty-headed Pothila." This monk had wisdom, and so he did not feel upset or insulted but thought that the Buddha wanted to teach him something by calling him "empty-headed."

So after his lecture one evening he took his alms bowl and robe and went to the forest without telling anyone. There he found a group of young monks meditating. He approached them, paid his respects, and said, "Please teach me how to meditate."

One of the young monks said, "Venerable sir, please do not embarrass me. You are an eminent teacher. Please ask another monk." So Pothila went to the next monk, and the next, but none of the monks wanted to teach the elder. All felt too shy. Finally he reached the youngest monk and repeated his plea.

"Please teach me how to meditate," he said, adding, "I will do anything you ask of me."

"Alright," consented the youngest novice monk. "There is a little pond full of mud. Get in the pond and listen to me very carefully."

So, dressed in his fine robes, the elder monk entered the muddy pond. As soon as Pothila entered the pond, the novice directed him to step out again and said, "Venerable sir, suppose there is an anthill with six holes in it. Suppose a lizard crawls into the anthill. How are you going to catch him?"

The elder monk replied that he would close five of the six holes and wait until the lizard came out of the sixth hole.

"Similarly, venerable sir," said the novice monk, "if you restrain five of your six senses—eyes, ears, nose, tongue, and body—and keep your mind focused on your breath, you will notice how all of the aggregates—form, feelings, perceptions, thoughts, and consciousness—change. You will become aware that breath is changing and feeling is changing. As breath comes and goes through your nostrils, feeling arises and passes away. Your attention on the breath and your awareness of the breath changes. This awareness of impermanence opens the door to insight into the reality that everything is unsatisfactory and there is no permanent entity called a self. Eventually your mind will become calm and peaceful, and you will gain concentration. Concentration deepens your insight into the attainment of liberation."[4]

And so gradually this elder monk, who knew so much Dhamma, learned how to practice and saw what was happening within himself. Practicing this way and withdrawing his senses, he attained enlightenment very quickly. After this, the Buddha never again called him "empty-headed."

Dependent origination is like a domino effect: everything gradually falls when one link topples. It starts with ignorance, and so with the dissolution of ignorance all the steps of dependent origination leading to sorrow, lamentation, pain, grief, and despair disappear as well. Therefore, understanding ignorance and how to end it irreversibly is the way to live a life free from suffering.

Ignorance is a vast subject, but in brief it means not knowing. In the Pali texts it is invariably defined as not knowing the four noble truths. In *The Discourse on Dependent Origination*, the Buddha describes each step of dependent origination as follows:

> And what, bhikkhus, is ignorance? Not knowing suffering, not knowing the origin of suffering, not knowing the cessation of suffering, not knowing the way leading to the cessation of suffering. This is called ignorance.[5]

Upon hearing this, you may ask what is noble in these four truths, in suffering, and in the cause of suffering. And there is nothing noble in suffering or in its cause. What is noble is the truth behind these four statements.

From the moment we are born our bodies and life conditions keep changing. Our inability to control, inhibit, or even anticipate the perpetually changing situations in life causes us to reject, object to, and mentally oppose them. This mental attitude stems from the inability to understand impermanence. For one lacking the right view of impermanence, everything that is impermanent entails suffering. Pleasure and pain are both impermanent. When pain subsides, pleasure arises. However, pleasure is always subdued compared to the experience of pain; the mind tends to predominantly notice pain. This resistance to pain and attachment to pleasure due to the lack of understanding and acceptance of impermanence causes stress, tension, and despair—in other words, suffering. Ignoring the reality of impermanence is ignorance, which results in suffering.

From our early childhood we reject whatever displeases us. All throughout our lives we ignore the reality of change, constantly living in uncertainty about what our future holds. There are always unexpected events that occur in our lives, and these should wake us up to the real nature of life. When we know the reality of existence we are always mindful, alert, and prepared to accept the inevitable and unexpected occurrences. This is living in wisdom, the opposite of ignorance.

All conditioned things are endowed with three characteristics: impermanence, un-satisfactoriness, and nonself. We all experience these. No one could argue with the fact that suffering is a common experience in life. But do we know how to overcome it, and can we actually do it? If so, then why don't we? Due to ignorance, we are unable to see that these characteristics constitute the very fabric of all conditioned things. We delude ourselves by thinking that things are permanent, imbued with permanence, that they'll last forever, and that they are the source of our happiness. But that is not their nature, and therefore we suffer. Because things are impermanent, they cannot be fully satisfactory. And they cannot be considered as having a self, for the very notion of self implies permanence.

All existence, in all three times—past, present, and future—is endowed with suffering. Birth, old age, sickness, and death; separation from what we love and association with what we hate; not getting what we want and getting what we don't want—these are all forms of dissatisfaction. They are all suffering.

So what is the cause of suffering? Greed and its insatiability is the cause of suffering. When we try to satisfy our greed, we quickly find out how difficult this is. Any attempt at fully satisfying greed can only be met with stress, anxiety, and unsatisfactoriness. The Buddha used words like "sorrow, lamentation, pain, grief, and despair" to describe the futility of satisfying greed. But no matter how many words you coin, you can never fully capture the whole meaning of the phrase "The insatiability of greed is suffering," which implies the cause of suffering as well as its end. This means that when greed is totally eliminated from our minds, suffering ends. When one doesn't know the first of the four noble truths, suffering, then one certainly doesn't know the other three. Therefore, to end suffering one must first understand it. This can be achieved not by reading or memorizing books but by deep introspection and right understanding. One must learn to see things as they really are. Words have limitations and can never carry the full meaning of a direct experience. It's just like going to the Grand Canyon: I can describe it to you, but you cannot experience its majesty unless you see it for yourself.

Nothing happens in isolation: when this arises, this arises. But being gripped by ignorance, we are not able to see this. And therefore ignorance is not knowing dependent origination.

Ignorance of Extremes

We have introduced the two potent factors that keep us bound in samsara. On the one hand, ignorance blocks our view, preventing us from having correct understanding and awareness of reality. On the other hand, greed grips us by our desires and has the characteristics of binding or clinging.[6]

As long as ignorance and greed exist within us, it is not possible to put an end to suffering. Interestingly, when the Buddha delivered his first sermon, he did not use the word *ignorance*; instead, he used *craving*. Craving for sensual pleasures (always referred to in the plural) is self-indulgence, while craving for the opposite of sensual pleasures is self-mortification. Both of these extremes must be avoided. It is only when one understands this point properly through the practice of insight meditation that one can be free from suffering. Let us examine why.

The Buddha used five expressions to describe the qualities of sense pleasures: very low, ordinary, pertaining to one who does not know the Dhamma, not noble, and endowed with harm. This is the very nature of self-indulgence, and yet people like it because they don't see the danger in self-indulgence. Such is ignorance, which keeps beings bound in samsara. Going around and around in samsara, perpetuating their existence, enjoying this life, beings pass away wishing to continue their enjoyments in futures lives. Living unmindfully, sunk deep in ignorance, prey to the pleasures of the senses, they prepare themselves for rebirth in lower realms no matter how unappealing such destinations might seem. When the current life ends, driven by delight in sensual pleasures, one wishes to be born again to continue sense enjoyment. This endless cycle keeps spinning for one who does not know the Dhamma. The drive to pursue sense enjoyment is common in the animal realm, where the minds of beings are completely gripped by ignorance. On the other hand, one who knows and follows the Dhamma has little interest in sense enjoyment and becomes a noble person—that is, one on the path to attain liberation from suffering.

But ordinary beings remain in ignorance because they do not see the harm and danger that it causes. This is due to distorted perception. Because of ignorance, they think that what is unpleasant is pleasant, that something that does not have self does have self, and that the pleasure they experience is permanent. Some people even glorify this desire and call it eternal love. People with this type of view are called eternalists.

They believe in perpetual existence, wanting to exist forever in order to enjoy sense pleasures unceasingly. They perpetuate the notion of a permanent self and sink deeper and deeper into ignorance. Self-indulgence is therefore an extreme to be avoided.

Once you are tied to the yoke of sensual pleasures, it is very difficult to get out of it because you cannot see their inherent danger. You may question whether living without sensual pleasures is even possible, using all kinds of arguments such as the necessity of sensual pleasures for having children, maintaining population growth, and so on. You work very hard to enjoy sensual pleasures, but along with pleasure comes pain—you buy one, and you get one free. Along with pleasure, you get pain for free. Remember, the Buddha said that not getting what one wants is suffering and that even getting what one wants is suffering.

So we are stuck in this trap. Once you get something or someone you desire, you must endure an enormous amount of pain and suffering. This is because greed and ignorance work together. The Buddha said that ignorance is a hindrance and craving is a fetter. While one is blinded by ignorance one is also tied to sensual pleasures. The outcome of this is undoubtedly suffering. To be free of this trap, we must understand it clearly.

Let us take, for example, an inanimate object such as a car, a house, or anything that is an object of strong desire. Suppose that you have wished to get a fancy car for a long time. Once you acquire it you have to pay insurance for it, maintain it, and take care of every little detail related to that car. And when something breaks, you have to repair it. All of this does not come for free! You have to pay for all these things. And if it is an expensive car you have to work hard to earn enough money to repay the car loan. All this can keep you engaged and busy, leaving you without much time for yourself. You must work, earn money to pay the bills, and then work, earn money, pay bills . . . all because you got what you wanted.

On the other hand, not getting what you want is suffering, because you don't see the drawbacks in obtaining it and obsessing over it, sometimes even at the expense of your health. Here again, this suffering is due to greed and ignorance.

The other extreme is self-mortification. A person who has acquired some degree of understanding of the danger of sensual pleasures may decide to abandon them. This is the case for some monks, nuns, laymen, and laywomen, who, having given up all sensual pleasures to become ascetics, think that the way to liberate themselves from suffering is through torturing the body. Prompted by a strong desire to liberate oneself as quickly as possible, one may adopt extreme ascetic practices, thinking that one shouldn't eat as much as others or get enough sleep but should go on practicing yoga or meditation at the expense of one's health. This extreme has its basis in ignorance and desire, and individuals who practice self-mortification do not understand the danger.

The Buddha learned this for himself. Before realizing that this was not the way to liberate himself from suffering, Siddhatta Gotama tortured his body for six years, which reduced him to a mere skeleton. After achieving enlightenment, the Buddha described the practice as painful, not noble, and dangerous. Those who do not understand the uselessness of these two extremes follow them, but the Buddha taught us the middle path, a way out of suffering that avoids them.

Extremes are not solely based on lifestyles such as self-indulgence and self-mortification but also can take the form of ideology or ways of thinking. The beliefs that everything exists or that nothing exists are extremes based on wrong understanding. All phenomena arise (appear) and fall (disappear). Seeing only the arising (the coming of all things into existence) is one extreme, and seeing only the falling (their dissolution) is another. Nihilism causes the angst of being annihilated, conveying the notion of absolute destruction. It can also lead one to live an immoral life, thinking that there are no repercussions for one's actions in another life. On the other hand eternalists believe that by perpetually performing meritorious deeds one would be reborn under increasingly better conditions life after life. But due to various circumstances and conditions this is not always possible, and so there is no guarantee that one would be reborn in a better state from one life to the next. What is certain is that going from life to life leads to endless suffering, as each life has its load of sorrows. One who avoids these extremes and sees both the arising and the falling will have right understanding and see things without ignorance.

Wrong view is a type of extreme that comes from a lack of understanding and leads to wrong thought, wrong speech, wrong action, wrong effort, wrong mindfulness, and wrong concentration. It is a distorted view that sees what is impermanent as permanent and what is not self as self. Such views are wrong for the simple reason that they do not bring peace, happiness, and the expected result of liberation from suffering. Some people are not even aware of their own suffering; such chronic skeptics are so attached to their views that they are incapable of giving them up. Those who hold on to wrong views are prone to acting in a way that does not produce peace, happiness, and liberation. Lost in the snares of wrong view, they are totally unaware that it will bring them harm. Wrong view is therefore the cause of much suffering because it keeps one bound in the cycle of samsara.

The Buddha clearly explained this point with the similes of the snake and the raft.[7] If a man wants to catch a snake to extract its poison and catches it by its tail, it will turn around and bite him, causing death or severe sickness. Similarly, a person with wrong view can harm himself and even others. Just as the snake can seriously injure and possibly even kill the person who tries to catch it by the wrong end, misunderstanding the Dhamma can cause harm to oneself and others. Millions of people can be misled because of wrong view and misunderstandings. This doesn't just happen in this life; it goes on in the next, and the next. Due to ignorance, those holding wrong views do not even understand that they have wrong views at all and therefore perpetuate their suffering in this life and potentially many future lives.

Just so with a raft. One cannot hold on to a raft so tightly that one cannot row—just tightly enough not to fall off. Similarly when you learn the Dhamma you must know how to use it correctly. Grab too tightly and you become a religious fanatic, too loosely and you don't practice it and cannot use it. Therefore, without grasping or holding on too loosely, you find the middle way to practice the Dhamma. And in the end you must let go of the raft once the river has been crossed. In the simile of the raft the Buddha asks if a person should keep carrying a raft on their shoulders after using it to cross a river. The answer is of course no. In the same way, after practicing the Dhamma and attaining enlightenment, one relinquishes all attachments, not holding on to anything, not even the Dhamma.

Using the weapon of wisdom to avoid extremes, one should not get stuck to one's attainments and must let go of them too. When you have made progress in spiritual practice do not stay there. Let it go and continue your journey onward. If you have any desire to hold on to your attainment, you have not yet won the battle against your defilements. Therefore, the real winning is letting go of whatever achievements or spiritual gain you have obtained and continuing toward the ultimate goal of liberation.

THE ROOTS OF IGNORANCE

Ignorance and greed constitute the roots of our suffering. But ignorance does not arise by itself. It depends on and is sustained by other factors, called influxes (Pali *asava*). Although "influx" is an appropriate translation, it does not convey the whole meaning of *asava*, which means "fermentation," referring to organic material buried in the ground to ferment. Alcohol can be produced this way, and while this can give you a very strong kick, it can also get you intoxicated.

Asavas have that effect on us in samsara, intoxicating us and drowning us. We brew the influxes of ignorance through our eyes, ears, body, and mind as well as our behaviors, and they ferment and remain in our subconscious minds. In samsara we keep harping on the same things, bringing so many unwholesome thoughts to our minds. Someone who keeps thinking of stealing, for example, will surely develop the underlying tendency to steal.

There are four kinds of influxes: sense desires, wrong views, becoming, and ignorance. We will talk about sense desires and how to overcome them in later chapters. The second is wrong views, which make it difficult for us to understand the Dhamma. Therefore, right understanding is necessary to overcome wrong view. The third influx, the desire for becoming, is called *bhavasava*, which comes from a Pali term meaning "wish." This desire for becoming—the renewing of a particular state—makes us cling tightly to existence. We are never the same from one moment to the next, but our existence is renewed based on the conditions of the previous moment.

Lastly, ignorance is known as the root influx because it obstructs a clear view of the nature of conditioned things and thereby leads to wrong views regarding the impermanence of all things. Suppose someone with an unpurified mind sees a beautiful lake. After enjoying the beautiful scenery they decide to live there, thinking that the pleasantness they experience now would last forever once they have a house right by the lake. And so they go to great lengths to buy an expensive house there, incurring debt and much stress. But after a while the pleasant experience that led them to make the rash decision fades away. Then one day a tropical storm hits the area, and what started with a pleasant experience and irrational clinging to it ends in sheer disappointment.

Underneath the asavas is another layer of unrefined defilements called *anusaya* in Pali, which means "sleeping with." Sleeping in the subconscious mind, these underlying tendencies seem almost dormant, and yet they support the influxes, which in turn support ignorance. There are seven underlying tendencies of ignorance: aversion or anger, hatred, lust or greed, wrong views, conceit, desire for being, and—importantly—ignorance itself. Being both an influx and an underlying tendency, ignorance works in conjunction with the underlying tendencies by blocking our right view and right understanding. Therefore, ignorance itself is a support for ignorance.

THE HINDRANCES

In addition to the series of underlying tendencies and influxes already discussed, there are five hindrances that support and nourish ignorance: greed (desire), anger, sleepiness and drowsiness, restlessness and worry, and doubt. Ignorance does not work alone; it receives help from all these defilements. These hindrances are obstacles that we also encounter during our meditation practice, and so let us spend a few moments describing how hindrances arise in meditation.

In the course of our lives, we collect a vast amount of information through our six senses. Most of this information gets stored in our memory banks, and due to the complexity of the human brain, these memories are quite vivid. Just imagine the amount of data we have stored in our brains over decades. Suppose that we start meditating at the age of thirty. We would not be starting with a clean slate; over thirty years, we would have seen, heard, smelled, tasted, touched, and thought so many things. Most of these impressions are stored in the mind.

Whenever the mind grabs on to something, even if it is for a few seconds, it is always because of desire. This is because desire triggers the act of seeing, hearing, smelling, tasting, touching, and thinking about the object of interest. The nature of desire is to glue on or stick to something. The longer we focus our attention on an object, the stronger its impression on the mind and its imprint on our memory. When we sit to meditate, we are not sitting with a blank mind but with countless things in our memory. Hence, when we first start a meditation practice, as soon as we try to quiet the mind and focus on one simple thing like the breath, many thoughts and mental impressions begin to surface. First, traumatic experiences in life resurface; in many cases, these are childhood experiences.

As these experiences resurface, hindrances promptly manifest. This is how desire and hatred arise in the mind, which can give rise to all kinds of attachments and thoughts of sense pleasures. We can get lost in thoughts about that new car we'd like to get or what we'd like to eat for breakfast. All these thoughts of sense pleasures can keep us distracted for a long time and cause us to waste a significant portion of our meditation session. Sleepiness arises when everything calms down. And restlessness can suddenly arise as a hindrance when we remember something from the past or when we project ourselves into the future. Doubt arises in the mind when we begin to question if we can succeed in our meditation practice. Some people give up meditating because of wrong meditation, wrong mindfulness, and wrong concentration. When our approach to meditation is consistently wrong then inevitably confusion and doubt follows, and we will eventually give up the practice altogether.

This, in a nutshell, is how hindrances enter our meditation practice. And it all depends on how much attention we have paid to sensorial and mental objects, the extent of our attachment to them, and the strength of impressions of enjoyment or hatred. The hindrances depend on these factors; they don't arise without any causes, independently. They can all be traced to the aforementioned causes.

THE FETTERS

In this section we will discuss the ten fetters that keep us bound in samsara. The first five are weightier than the latter five and include personality view, doubt, the belief that one can be liberated from suffering by following or performing rituals, greed for sensual pleasures, and hatred. The first three must be overcome to attain the first stage of liberation, and the next two attenuated to progress toward the second stage of liberation. The five latter fetters are all lighter than the first and are gradually overcome when one progresses toward full enlightenment: greed for fine material existence, greed for immaterial existence, conceit, restlessness, and ignorance.

People often become offended and upset when we talk about the nonexistence of self. Some find the Buddha's teaching to be marvelous and ethical but have a tough time accepting his exposition on nonself. However, understanding nonself is essential for liberating the mind from suffering, and lacking this understanding is the first fetter: personality view, the notion of self in various forms and guises. There are many ways in which this fetter manifests: believing that the five aggregates of body (form), feelings, perceptions, thoughts, and consciousness are with self; that self is in the aggregates; that the aggregates are in self; or that the aggregates are identical to self.

The prevalent strong attachment to the belief in a permanent self or soul causes a fear of annihilation when people first hear the Buddha's teaching on nonself. They come to the erroneous conclusion that the Buddha is talking about total annihilation. He certainly was not advising anybody to destroy life but was instead talking about the nonexistence of a permanent self. The Buddha's teaching is about the absolute destruction of suffering and the greed, hatred, and delusion that cause it.

Even during the Buddha's own time, this teaching on impermanence in relation to a self was misconstrued and he had to clarify its meaning. Some could not see this truth even while living in his monastery. In the Pali suttas, we come across the story of a monk named Sati, who thought that it is the same self, the same consciousness, that goes from life to life. In time the Buddha learned the Venerable Sati was spreading this pernicious view and called him into his presence. After verifying that the monk was dead set on his pernicious view, the Buddha reprimanded him and explained with an enlightening discourse that this is wrong view. Ignorance, and attachment to the belief of a permanent self, is so hard to crack that even some monks who lived near the Buddha fell into wrong view.

The second fetter is doubt about the Buddha, Dhamma, and Sangha as well as the moral and ethical principles laid out by the Buddha. One may be deluded into thinking that liberation from all suffering can be attained even without observing these moral principles. At the time of the Buddha a monk named Arittha claimed that eradicating the defile-ments was unnecessary for liberation because the hindrances described by the Buddha as such are not really obstacles to liberation. This is called a pernicious view, and it arises in the mind due to not understanding the truth as a result of ignorance.

The Buddha reprimanded him for this wrong view and gave many illustrations to correct it. Using many similes, he explained how sensual pleasures provide little gratification and much despair to those who fall prey to them. They are akin to a skeleton, a pit of coals, a grass torch, borrowed good that must be returned after a while, or a blood-smeared bone that a dog chews on, never getting nourished and damaging his gums. The Buddha's teaching must be followed exactly and without cut-ting corners. Thinking that shortcuts will lead to liberation is also due to ignorance. Even during the Buddha's lifetime some monks thought that sensual pleasures would not be a hindrance to spiritual progress, and so they argued against the rules laid out by the Buddha aimed at curtailing greed for sensual pleasures. But their spiritual progress remained stalled until they understood the purpose of these rules and started following them. As a result, doubt in the Buddha's teaching and in their own prac-tice started to fade away, until it was no more.

Doubt can arise as a hindrance but also as a fetter. It is important to understand the difference between the two, for a fetter is a far more deeply rooted mental state than a hindrance. While a hindrance can be temporarily eliminated, a fetter can take a long time to root out. A fetter is like an entire network of deep underground roots; the shoots coming out of the ground are like a hindrance. Therefore, when doubt arises as a hindrance it is more readily visible and easier to remove than when it arises as a deeply rooted fetter and obstructs our understanding of the Dhamma. Moreover, as a fetter it blocks our path to the first stage of liberation—stream-entry.

When we have doubts, we are perplexed, confused, and cannot pro-ceed. Doubt is a stumbling block that eventually leads to skepticism.

Skeptics typically do not accept any answer to any question. When you try to answer their first question, instead of trying to understand the answer they are already thinking of another question. This is because they are not interested in your answer; they just want to ask questions. Therefore, in many ways doubt is unwholesome, unprofitable, and to be overcome.

However, doubt has a positive side as well—optimistic doubt. A person genuinely interested in understanding something should be encouraged to ask questions on the topic that they are investigating. It is also essential for a Dhamma practitioner intent on understanding subtle points of the teachings to ask questions of those who have mastered them in order to clear his or her doubts. This kind of doubt is healthy and wholesome. Wholesome doubt implies asking questions with the intention of learning the Dhamma in order to free the mind from doubt.

And once the mind is free from doubt, faith develops. Faith with understanding is wholesome faith, not blind faith. It is faith supported by understanding regarding the Buddha, the Dhamma, and the Sangha. This is the faith of an individual who has attained the stage of stream-entry. Unwholesome doubt must be overcome, and wholesome doubt must be maintained, supported, and encouraged. The Buddha's teachings are meant to be accepted not on blind faith but with insightful questioning, inquiring, and even doubting until we grasp them with full clarity.

The third fetter is the belief that one can be liberated from suffering through rites and rituals. For example, some think that lighting a lamp on certain auspicious occasions can bring good luck and remove obstacles to liberation. Some may think this will remove the darkness of ignorance, allowing wisdom to dawn. And people observe many rites and rituals merely out of habit. The Buddha discouraged people from such observances, for attachment to them is a sure way to hinder or even to block the attainment of liberation completely.

When people spend time on rituals, thinking that such things can lead to liberation, they don't go to the heart of the matter. Believing that these practices are sufficient, they stop putting effort in the correct practice, which involves the noble eightfold path of right understanding, intention, speech, action, livelihood, effort, mindfulness, and concentration. Thus, solely adhering to rites and rituals is a waste of time. You have a limited lifespan, and every moment must be used wisely to attain liberation. If you lose this precious short time on rituals, when will you find the time to practice the Dhamma? One day you realize that rituals have not brought you one iota of wisdom to liberate yourself from suffering, and then you let go of them.

There are various types of greed: desire for sensual pleasures, which is the fourth fetter, desire for material things, desire for thoughts, and even desire for the Dhamma. In order to attain liberation we should not cling to anything, not even the Dhamma, for clinging to the Dhamma has its dangers too. It can make people inflexible, thinking that they are a beacon of truth and that everyone else is wrong. Such an attitude stems from desire and ignorance.

An excuse commonly used to justify the need for sensual desire is that it is necessary for the continuation of the human species. Some even go as far as claiming that because of this need, laypeople cannot practice the Dhamma. This certainly isn't true. As long as there is a correct understanding of the Dhamma, anyone can practice it.

There are many stories in our Buddhist Pali texts about laypeople attaining enlightenment while enjoying their household lives. One such tale involves a woman called Milayandaka, who lived near the Buddha's monastery. One day she invited Ananda, the Buddha's attendant, for lunch and told him of the spiritual attainments of her father and uncle:

> Bhante, my father, Purana, began to observe celibacy when I was born. When he passed away, the Buddha said that he had attained the second level of enlightenment, *sakadagami*, the stage called "once-returning." My father's brother, on the other hand, did not give up sensual pleasures. He lived a

householder's life, enjoying sensual pleasures. And when he passed away, the Buddha said that he too had attained the second level of enlightenment. I cannot understand how both of them attained the second level of enlightenment: one was celibate, and the other was not.[8]

Upon his return to the monastery, Ananda related this entire conversation to the Buddha, who said that Purana was a pious and faithful person who observed celibacy. This rendered his mind calm, without the agitation and excitements resulting from sensual pleasures. As a result, he was able to attain the second level of enlightenment by overcoming the first three fetters. His brother, on the other hand, was a wise person who knew how to balance his life, how and when to practice meditation, and how to live without becoming attached to his household life. He too practiced meditation and saw impermanence in sensual pleasures, and he understood the inherent danger in them. Seeing impermanence, he developed his mindfulness, insight, and wisdom and attained the second level of enlightenment as well.

Another inspiring story is that of Lady Visakha, a rich and generous woman who had much faith in the Buddha. When she encountered the Buddha at the age of seven she attained the first level of enlightenment, stream-entry. And when she became a young woman, she married and had many children.

The fifth fetter is hatred. It is another mighty obstacle to attaining liberation. Hatred can grip our minds so firmly that it is difficult for most of us to let go of it. It can even take the form of self-hatred and is more insidious than desire. We can see desire coming and going, but much more effort is required to overcome hatred. The hateful state of mind can be compared to boiling water, as the boiling makes it hard to see the bottom of the vessel.

Hatred confuses the mind, rendering it completely incapable of clear thinking and reasoning. When our minds are muddled up with anger or hatred, we cannot speak skillfully, our feelings are disturbed, and a burning sensation grips our hearts. This is why it is called the fire of anger.

And this is why the practice of *metta* (loving friendliness) is so important. The benefits of this practice are numerous. It is said that the *metta* practitioner will not be affected by fire, by poison, or by any weapon. But this cannot be taken literally. Figuratively, these refer to greed, hatred, and delusion. Fear, doubt, greed, hatred, and ignorance are all fire; they burn and consume us day by day. And therefore hatred is a powerful fetter that requires our utmost effort to be eradicated.

Aside from these five, there are five additional fetters that must be overcome to attain full liberation. They are greed for fine material existence, greed for immaterial existence, conceit, restlessness, and ignorance.

Greed for fine material or immaterial existence stems from the realization that the body is prone to sickness, old age, and all the pains and aches that come with aging. Many discomforts affect the body: cold, heat, nature's calls, and so on. When the weather gets cold, you can put on warmer clothes, but you cannot get rid of the cold temperature outside. We get cold, then warm, too warm, and then cold again. We never stay comfortable. And then there are the feelings of hunger and thirst that keep tormenting our bodies, perpetually calling our attention to satisfy them. We can temporarily quench our thirst, but sure enough, later on we'll be thirsty again.

As long as we have a body, we must constantly tend to its needs. This is why some people think that attaining a fine material existence would be better than having a gross material body. Wishing to attain the stage of fine material existence—or taking it even further, immaterial existence—they meditate with good intentions. But here again there is desire, the desire to exist in a fine material form in order to be free from the constraints of caring for the gross body.

Greed is a deeply rooted mental state that is so persistent that it remains even after the third stage of enlightenment as a residue of conceit, restlessness, and worry. Conceit is the eighth fetter, a faint residue of the notion

"I am," which is different from viewing the aggregates as self. To get rid of this fetter we must have an undiluted, clear, and perfect understanding of impermanence. It is only with a complete awareness of impermanence that one can eradicate the pernicious notion of self by learning to look at oneself introspectively and without any bias whatsoever.

To understand the nature of this fetter, let us recall the story of the Venerable Khemaka as related in *The Discourse on Khemaka*.[9] The Venerable Khemaka was sick, afflicted, and so senior monks sent the Venerable Dasaka to enquire about him. Throughout their exchange, mediated by the messenger Dasaka, the elderly monks tried to determine if the Venerable Khemaka saw anything as self or belonging to self. This exchange went on for a while until eventually the Venerable Khemaka went to see the other monks himself despite his illness. He explained that although he had let go of the five lower fetters and that he did not view any of the five aggregates subject to clinging as self, he had not yet relinquished the notion "I am" regarding the aggregates. Even though he was not attached to any of the aggregates and did not regard any of them as "I am this," the notion "I am" had not yet vanished in him in relation to the five aggregates subject to clinging. While using the simile of a lotus flower in searching for the source of its scent, he explained that the scent of the flower is not located in any part of the components of the flower. In the same way, he did not view the notion "I am" as belonging to any of the aggregates. However, there remained in him a residual conceit, a desire, and an underlying tendency of "I am" that had not been uprooted.

As he reflected on the remainder of the notion "I am" in him, he presented the following analogy to his fellow monks: Suppose a soiled cloth were washed with a certain kind of detergent. The cloth would smell of the detergent, and the scent of the cloth is just like the remaining notion "I am." In order to remove this scent, you would put it in a perfumed box. Eventually, the cloth would take the scent of the perfume in the box, and the smell of detergent would be gone.

As he spoke these words, the Venerable Khemaka understood that with the correct contemplation of the rise and fall of the aggregates, the notion "I am" would also vanish. The scent of the cloth was impermanent. The smell of detergent appeared and disappeared. In the same way, with correct insight into impermanence, the last residue of ignorance, the notion "I am," vanishes because we are able to see that everything is constantly changing so rapidly that nothing can exist permanently, not even "I." Having seen this clearly for himself, the Venerable Khemaka let go of the concept "I am." And, not clinging to anything, he became fully liberated. As ignorance completely vanished from his mind, the Venerable Khemaka became one of the arahants, as did all the elderly monks listening to his discourse. Wherever there is clinging, there is ignorance; and where there is ignorance, there is clinging. Full liberation is the complete cessation of the notion of "I" without any remainder of greed.

The ninth fetter is restlessness, which renders the meditator's mind restless in anticipation of the final attainment. This is not the mundane agitation that an unenlightened person might feel during the day or the hindrance of restlessness experienced during meditation. It is instead the shattering realization that our conception regarding the nature of existence was wrong all along. To overcome this fetter, he or she must use more mindfulness to balance all the factors of enlightenment, to be examined later in this chapter.

The Last Fetter

The tenth fetter is ignorance, the ridgepole of this house of suffering. A ridgepole is a horizontal pole along the ridge of a roof into which the rafters are fastened, and if the ridgepole is shattered the entire house collapses. Similarly, when this last fetter collapses rebirth comes to an end. In the *Dhammapada* we can read the beautiful words uttered by the Buddha where he uses this image to express the glory of the dawn of his enlightenment:

> Through many births
> I have wandered on and on,
> Searching for, but never finding,
> The builder of [this] house.
> To be born again and again is suffering.
> House-builder, you are seen!
> You will not build a house again!
> All the rafters are broken,
> The ridgepole destroyed;
> The mind, gone to the Unconstructed,
> Has reached the end of craving![10]

According to this stanza, the Buddha was looking for the cause of birth in each of his many lives, thinking about why rebirth occurs, "seeking the builder of this house." Here, "this house" refers to the body, which houses many parts within its parameters. Most of us do not question why we are born, live our lives, and die. Repeated birth is indeed suffering! Birth is suffering not just in this life but in every life, and in each one the Buddha kept on trying to understand why.

Finally, his long and arduous research paid off. He found "the builder of [this] house"—craving, the cause of rebirth. In saying "House-builder, you are seen! You will not build a house again!" the Buddha proclaimed that craving cannot hide any longer. The rafters are defilements and passions, and in breaking the rafters the Buddha eradicated all defilements. It was while searching for the cause of birth in samsara that the Buddha saw dependent origination, with ignorance being the first step in the formula.

OVERCOMING INFLUXES

We have discussed earlier that the four influxes of sense desires, becoming, ignorance, and wrong views are the supporting factors of ignorance. And so when we get rid of influxes, ignorance will disappear in turn. But how do we get rid of them? How do we start? Several methods are available to us, such as seeing, restraining, using, abandoning, avoiding, and removing. In this section we will look at each method in turn.

First, we must overcome the influxes by seeing, taking an impartial look at things as they really are. A lack of clarity and impartiality while seeing can lead to several useless self-reflections formulated in series of unbeneficial questions. Regarding the past, one might think, "Was I in the past? Was I not in the past? How was I in the past? What was I in the past? What did I become in the past?" In the present, one might think, "Am I? Am I not? What am I? Who am I? Where did I come from? Where will I go after?" Then in the future, "Shall I be? Shall I not be? How shall I be? What shall I be? What shall I become in the future?" Note that the person thinks in terms of "I" in each case. Thinking "how was I in the past," the person conceptualizes an unchanging, permanent, eternal "I." As long as this notion of a permanent "I" remains in the mind, ignorance is also present. Referring to a permanent entity continuing from past to present to future constitutes wrong view, which leads to a plethora of mental proliferations that inundate the mind with "I, I, I, I, I."

When we listen to conversations between people, we notice that the word most often used is this one single letter: *I*. Of course, we must use it to communicate; even the Buddha used the word *I*. But it is the use of the first-person pronoun *I* to represent a permanent, eternal ego or unchanging entity that is the problem. Employing it in this sense is supported by the influx of ignorance. It is due to a lack of clear comprehension, the inability to see things as they really are.

So what exactly do we mean when we talk about seeing clearly? It means that our understanding of impermanence must be clear. It is only when impermanence is fully grasped with deep insight and clear comprehension that a person becomes a stream enterer, one who has overcome the view of the aggregates as self. When one sees impermanence—the arising and falling of all phenomena—clearly within oneself with deep insight, one gains concentration and can liberate the mind from the notion of a permanent self.

The next step in overcoming influxes is by restraining. Restraining our eyes, ears, nose, tongue, body, and mind is just like putting on a filter. In this day and age many people wear filters in the form of face masks to prevent viruses from entering their bodies. Similarly, we can wear mental masks to prevent influxes from entering our minds.

There are four well-trained gatekeepers ready to protect us from influxes: mindfulness, effort, morality, and wisdom. Mindfulness is paramount and is the foundation of our spiritual progress. Effort is applied to prevent unwholesome influxes from entering our minds through our eyes, ears, nose, tongue, body, and mind. If an unwholesome mental state has become established, we apply effort the very moment that it slips into our mind, remove it, and replace it with wholesome states of mind: thoughts of friendliness, compassion, generosity, and appreciative joy. Once these states are established, we use effort again to maintain them. Morality, or following ethics, means that whenever influxes enter our minds we become immediately aware of our commitment to abide by the moral principles of the precepts. Lastly we must be wise to see the danger of these influxes. They intoxicate, confuse, and bewilder us and make us unable to see the truth. This is how we must train ourselves.

The third way of overcoming influxes is using—that is, using things in a way that helps our efforts to eliminate suffering. This method is strongly recommended for monastics, the monks and nuns who observe monastic principles. In their case, this applies especially to the four requisites of clothing, food, shelter, and medicines. However, the practice of overcoming influxes by using appropriately can also be extended to laypeople.

Monastics use robes, and while using them, they practice the following mindful reflection: "I use this robe mindfully, with mindful reflection to ward off cold, heat, gadflies, and mosquitoes and to cover my nakedness." This is the sole purpose for wearing robes. It isn't a particular kind of fashion. Monastics don't replace them yearly; there is no new monastic robes fashion coming to the market. This style is 2,600 years old, and monastics keep it for the rest of their lives. They use robes solely to protect themselves from the cold, the heat, insects, and the elements and to cover themselves. Wearing robes with this sole purpose in mind simplifies their lives and keeps the influxes of pride and greed from arising in their minds.

Similarly, monastics use food for the sole purpose of removing hunger while maintaining the self-control not to overeat. Before each meal, they recite the following verse: "I use this food not for play, nor as a game, nor for putting on weight, nor to make myself beautiful. I use this food in order to maintain this body so that I can practice the *brahmacharya* life."[11] This means to live a life based on the principles of the noble eightfold path without too much discomfort. Therefore, the only purpose of food is to maintain the body in order to practice the Dhamma. It isn't to build big, chiseled muscles to look more attractive. Food is simply viewed as medicine for the continuation of life. Just like our body, it is made up of four elements and is subject to decay. No matter how tasty the food is, it becomes unpleasant and unappealing as soon as it is consumed due to its impermanence. We should use our food while reflecting on this.

Similar reflections relate to shelter, the purpose of which is to protect us from heat, cold, and the elements, rather than glorify ourselves by living in rich houses. In the same way, we only use medicine to overcome the pain caused by certain diseases; our society is all too aware of the ravages caused by using pain medication for recreation. Of course these practices are not just for monks and nuns. Lay people should keep these in mind too as guidelines for how to live their lives. Using the requisites with these attitudes inhibits influxes from entering the mind.

The next method used to overcome influxes is abandoning, which requires great effort because abandoning anything is not easy. Any kind of addiction, such as social media, video games, food, and drinks, produces spikes of the neurotransmitter dopamine in the brain. When the source of the addiction has been consumed, the dopamine level drops and one re-engages in the addiction to bring the dopamine level back up. Indulging the addiction changes the dopamine baseline so that one needs to increase the frequency of indulging to bring it back up. This produces a vicious cycle that makes giving up bad habits difficult. There are four kinds of right effort, one of which is abandoning what is unwholesome. Here we are discussing abandoning in particular the four influxes of greed, becoming, ignorance, and wrong view. When any of these influxes obsesses our minds we cannot see the truth. Therefore, in order to see clearly we must strive to overcome or abandon whatever unwholesome mental states arise.

Avoiding works as well for overcoming influxes. For example, we must avoid people who lead us astray and influence us to do unskillful things. In *The Discourse on the Supreme Blessings*, the Buddha said that not associating with fools is a blessing.[12] Foolish people destroy their own and others' spiritual lives by doing wrong things. And when we associate with them, our influxes increase. It is therefore better to avoid them by all means.

There are, however, inevitable circumstances when we cannot avoid the wrong company. Maybe you happen to live with someone who tries to bias your understanding and drag you along the wrong path by pulling you into their distorted views. You may become so tired of trying to convince them otherwise that you end up giving in to their persuasions. But as difficult as it is to practice avoiding people, we still have to earnestly try and free ourselves at the first available moment.

People who can lead us astray are not the only thing to avoid. Environments such as rough and dangerous areas, poisonous plants, wildlife, and so on, put us in perilous situations. Modern society has encountered many hardships in the form of epidemics, whether viral or drug related. Avoiding acts and situations contributing to the spread of these epidemics by using all necessary precautions greatly benefits us and others. People from all walks of life become victims of drug use by just trying them once under the influence of seemingly amicable and popular individuals.

In such cases the practice of avoiding would have prevented so much suffering, hardship, and heartache. And so whatever prevents us from cleansing, freeing, and fully liberating our minds must be avoided at all costs.

Lastly influxes are overcome by removing three kinds of unwholesome thoughts: sensual desire, anger, and wishing harm upon others. As discussed earlier, thoughts of sensual pleasure arise through our senses and the mind. Thoughts of sensual desire are therefore removed by cleansing the mind—that is, immediately becoming mindful of whatever sense-desire possesses and obsesses the mind. Once we are mindful, we understand that such thoughts are blocking our right understanding. We must not tolerate them and instead render them nonexistent in the mind with effort, promptly removing them to free the mind from influxes.

Similarly, when thoughts of anger arise through our eyes, ears, nose, tongue, body, and mind, we must be mindful of their presence and eradicate them. Thoughts of hurting others are forms of cruelty that manifest through words or physical acts. As soon as these thoughts arise we must immediately become mindful that they are fierce and harmful, not to be kept in the mind, and let go of them at once.

These six methods of overcoming influxes strengthen the mind for developing the factors of enlightenment, to be discussed in the next section.

The Seven Factors of Enlightenment

The seven factors of enlightenment are practiced for the cultivation of total liberation, arahantship. They are divided into two categories: active factors (investigation, effort, and joy) and passive factors (tranquility, concentration, and equanimity), with mindfulness being the balancing factor between them. Practicing these enlightenment factors develops insight into impermanence and thereby directs the mind to let go of its tendency to cling. Thus, greed fades away. Without greed, anger has no footing. When the mind sees things as they are, that it is inherently impermanent, it is no longer subject to delusion. One thus becomes wise and overcomes ignorance.

The first factor of enlightenment is mindfulness, which can be developed anywhere, anytime, whether sitting on a cushion for meditation, standing, walking, lying down, or having a conversation. We can develop it at any moment and become mindful of the three characteristics of existence—impermanence, unsatisfactoriness, and nonself—and thereby develop clear comprehension.

In order to reveal the truth of the three characteristics of existence, one should take an object of concentration. When selecting a particular domain, its intrinsic characteristics of impermanence, unsatisfactoriness, and nonself must be clear. These objects of investigation are described in the four foundations of mindfulness, to be discussed in chapter 7. To gain insight into the three characteristics of existence, the mind has to remain focused, alert, and ardent. Setting aside greed (attachment) and stress regarding the mind-body complex composed of the five aggregates, we should practice with zest and vigor in order to see the three characteristics of existence in our own body and mind. This requires developing the habit of paying total, undivided, mindful attention to whatever we are doing, whether it be thinking, speaking, or acting, which entails being heedful at every moment. To the extent that we are able to sustain this effort, we gain insight into the nature of impermanence, unsatisfactoriness, and nonself.

As our insight into the three characteristics of existence deepens, we notice their interconnectedness. With insight into impermanence, one gains an understanding of the unsatisfactoriness and nonself inherent to all conditioned phenomena. With an improved comprehension of the nature of dissatisfaction, one understands its connection to impermanence and nonself. In this way, developing discernment into any of the three characteristics of existence leads to a clearer understanding of the other two.

When we practice mindfulness, no matter how brief our practice is, it will all add up over time. It is just like drops of water rolling down from the top of a mountain; eventually the drops produce streams through tributaries, and small streams then grow into more significant rivers. Similarly, every time we practice mindfulness it adds to our total mindfulness factor of enlightenment. Therefore, we shouldn't think that we have to practice the mindfulness factor of enlightenment all at once, during just one or a few meditation sessions. Every fraction of mindfulness adds up to the mindfulness factor of enlightenment. This is how we can overcome the influxes of sense pleasures, becoming, ignorance, and wrong views, bit by bit.

The second factor of enlightenment is investigation of the Dhamma, which is necessary for spiritual progress. This means making the effort to read, discuss, memorize, and reflect on the Dhamma. We reflect on the meaning of the words we learn in Dhamma books or from our teachers, scrutinize their context, and think about how they apply to our lives and how to put them into practice in order to liberate ourselves from suffering. As mentioned earlier, in our study of the Dhamma we should not adopt an attitude of blind faith but rather be investigative. When we meet with friends to discuss the Dhamma, when we ask our teachers about the Buddha's teachings, or whenever we reflect on the Dhamma, we develop our investigation factor of enlightenment. This will lead in turn to the blossoming of wisdom in us.

The third factor of enlightenment is effort. We have already described the fourfold efforts involved in eradicating influxes: the efforts to prevent and abandon unwholesome states of mind and to arouse and develop wholesome ones. As we exert right effort our successes encourage us and clarity of understanding unfolds in us. We start seeing positive results in ourselves, and this motivates us to increase our efforts. This makes us very glad.

As a result, the fourth factor of enlightenment, joy, develops. Whenever we see the rising and falling of the aggregates, our wisdom, clear understanding, and insight begin to unfold. This too causes joy to arise. As our practice develops, along with investigation and effort, we begin to see how wonderful and marvelous the Dhamma is. We understand that it is the key to our liberation from suffering. And seeing that there is a genuine way out of suffering is a great source of joy indeed. This kind of joy has nothing to do with mundane happiness, which comes from excitement. When people have mundane joy, they may hug, kiss, jump up and down, sing, and work themselves up into a tizzy.

Spiritual joy, on the other hand, leads to a calm, relaxed, serene, and composed mind. This is called the tranquility factor of enlightenment. Anytime we see the Dhamma for ourselves and feel happy while meditating, discussing, and reading about the Dhamma, it is this kind of spiritual joy that we are experiencing. And this joy makes us tranquil, calm, relaxed, and peaceful.

The calm, relaxation, peacefulness, and tranquility resulting from the joy we experience when we attain insight into the Dhamma leads to the sixth factor of enlightenment, concentration. With concentration, we are able to see things clearly as they really are, and this brings equanimity to our minds. This is equanimity, the seventh and final factor of enlightenment, a supremely clear and pure state of mind that is attained during meditation.

When the mind gets excited rather than tranquil, the restlessness fetter is present. Restlessness as a hindrance is a negative state, but when we get close to attaining arahantship, it is not negative. Instead it is like trepidation or excitement when we finally see the light at the end of the tunnel after a long effort toward full enlightenment. To calm this excitement down, we employ mindfulness to balance the factors of investigation, effort, and joy with tranquility, concentration, and equanimity. In this way, all the calming factors are brought to mind, thereby enhancing tranquility, concentration, and equanimity.

THE FIVE AGGREGATES OF SUFFERING

At the beginning of this book we pointed out that we must see dependent origination within ourselves. Toward that end, our mind-body complex comprises five aggregates, or collections of many things: form, feeling, perception, thoughts (mental volitional formations), and consciousness. These components are the objects of this investigation. In this section we explain the connection between clinging and these aggregates and how this leads to suffering.

The Buddha called the sum total of our aggregates "the aggregates of suffering," "the five aggregates of clinging," or "the five aggregates subject to clinging." So, what is the difference between the five aggregates— form, feeling, and so on—and the five aggregates subject to clinging? The key difference is that as long as there is ignorance, there are the aggregates of clinging. And when all trace of ignorance is removed from the mind, there is no more clinging to the aggregates. While all people have the five aggregates of form, consciousness, and so on, most beings also have the latter. But fully enlightened beings, having removed their ignorance, do not have the five aggregates of clinging.

The five aggregates of clinging are the sources of our suffering, but we fail to grasp this fact due to ignorance. We cling to our body, feelings, perceptions, thoughts, and consciousness as an instinctive tendency. However, as long as we cling to them, we continue to suffer. So long as our body is healthy, young, strong, and energetic, we can utilize it to its full potential. We can run, exercise, develop big muscles, and embellish ourselves. In this way we cling to our body and grow attached to it. This is very natural. But the nature of the body isn't to stay youthful forever, no matter how many cosmetics we may inject into our skin. The longer we keep putting on a blindfold to avoid seeing this truth, the longer we remain in the darkness of ignorance.

If we think that the body is something solid, hard, permanent, eternal, a source of pride belonging to us, then we get deeply troubled whenever something unpleasant happens to it. We may become depressed, disappointed, and even grief stricken. When the body becomes sick, for instance, we feel depressed and disappointed because we can no longer do the activities we used to enjoy when we were healthy. But if we understand the impermanent nature of the body exactly as it is, then we simply use it, maintain it, support it, and sustain it for the continuation of life. And when it starts to age and decay, falls sick, and eventually dies, we understand that this is its nature and therefore remain perfectly unaffected by the changes it incurs.

The body is composed of four elements, giving us a sense of stability, hardness, solidity, and cohesion. But these characteristics are continuously changing. In fact, the body is like a clay pot, brittle and liable to break at any time. It is sensitive to the elements, too—even the bite of a tiny mosquito can cause it pain! This is the nature of the body, like a wound covered with skin; when the skin is removed, we have pain. And based on the texture of that skin we're called either beautiful or ugly, but in fact it is just a thin layer of tissue covering the body. We have a distorted perception of our physical forms. Everyone has identical body components, including this thin outer body covering that we call skin. And yet we can become very proud and attached to it. The prouder we are of our body, the more we suffer when it gets sick and ages. As a result, there is a huge amount of suffering related to it. Of course, we have to live with the body. But it must be understood that clinging to it is a source of great suffering and that the body will inevitably experience aches and pains. We cannot hide this fact under the rug and pretend that there is no suffering.

Just like the form aggregate, feeling has many components compounded together. They arise from what we perceive through our eyes, ears, nose, tongue, body, and mind. They can be pleasant, unpleasant, or neither pleasant nor unpleasant (neutral). These six kinds of feelings—one for each sense—are accompanied by underlying tendencies rooted in ignorance. When an unpleasant feeling arises, it does so with the underlying tendency of resentment. When a pleasant feeling arises, it does so with the underlying tendency of greed. And when a neutral feeling arises, it does so with the underlying tendency of confusion.

When a particular kind of feeling arises, transforms, and disappears, it is immediately followed by another kind of feeling, which upon ceasing is followed by yet another. Ignorance is the failure to see the entire sequence of feelings as they transform, from their arising, changing, passing away, arising again, changing, and passing away again. Not seeing this, one clings to pleasant feelings. And when these cease, as is their nature, they are replaced by unpleasant feelings, which produce a sentiment of aversion. This constant oscillation between grasping and averting produces a feverish state of mind that is accompanied by much suffering.

The third aggregate is perception. This is compared to a mirage, which can appear on a hot summer day and give the illusion of water at some distance. As we get closer to it, the water seems to move further away. And if we stop and turn around, the water seems to be behind us. We keep chasing it, and it looks like the water is chasing us. So in a way it is as if the water is deceiving us!

Things are not as they appear. There are all sorts of distorted perceptions related to the senses. In all cases, what we see first is distortion. From a distance, for example, a picture can look very beautiful. I remember when I went to Vatican City and saw Michelangelo's paintings in the Sistine Chapel. From a distance, they looked so lifelike that I mistook them for photographs. Modern technology and virtual reality also offer many examples of distorted perception. Misunderstanding modern technology could lead one to believe that all participants in a virtual meeting are actually sitting in the same room. This is one form of ignorance related to visual perception.

Thus distorted by perception, our mind operates in a similar fashion. We are usually unable to see the difference between wrong, distorted perception and clear, undistorted perception. Therefore, we get confused. But what we are really interested in understanding here are distorted perceptions in the context of the Dhamma—that is, whether a perception is distorted or undistorted, it is impermanent. This is the aspect of perception that we usually fail to see clearly or simply ignore. This pertains to our perceptions of the world around us and our responses to these perceptions. Let us consider other examples to further investigate this.

A concert is so thrilling to many people. But if you get really close to the stage, the sound is deafening. At first you rush to get to the concert, but when the loud sounds blast you, you want to put earplugs in. Many things seem so beautiful from a distance, but when we come closer they are not so beautiful, not so pleasant. We thought that sound would be pleasant. We ran toward it, got attached to it. But in the end, it is just a loud vibration that can end up giving us tinnitus if we're exposed to it for too long.

Our senses of taste and touch are distorted as well. We like junk food even though it is filled with non-nutritious and harmful content. Because of distorted taste and our attachment to it, we make wrong choices and consume things that harm our bodies. Other things appear to be very pleasing to touch, but eventually they too bring pain, suffering, and distorted thinking. We generally lack the insight to view this clearly, and therefore we experience the suffering arising from the five aggregates subject to clinging due to ignorance. But, if we do not cling to the aggregates, we can live a moderate, healthy, and happy life.

Furthermore, perceptions differ from person to person. When you and I look at the same thing, how I perceive it may not be exactly how you perceive it. Our perceptions depend on our individual mental state. Several factors are at play when we perceive objects, and we interpret objects according to our perception. Based on our interpretation, we increase our conceptual proliferations, which in turn keeps us in samsara.

The next aggregate is *sankharas*, or volitional formations. Volition, the faculty of using one's will, arises from desire. From the desire to own a new car, for example, there arises the volition to purchase it. If unchecked, the mind obsesses over the car, and clinging arises. Perhaps the car is out of our means or is an unnecessary purchase at this stage. But this clinging to the thought of the car occupies the mind to such a great extent that the danger of our choice is unseen. Hence, our clinging to these volitional formations brings about much suffering.

The last of the five aggregates is consciousness. There are many different types of consciousness that are amalgamated together to constitute this aggregate. We are not normally aware of these components and are therefore ignorant of our own consciousness. We will discuss consciousness in detail in chapter 3, but for now, let us understand how we cling to it.

Consciousness is the most vital aspect of our personality. At the same time, it is the most subtle aspect of our mind-body complex, an awareness that, when activated by a sensorial stimulus, projects in the direction of that stimulus via the sense doors. Consciousness can also be activated by a nonsensorial stimulus that is purely mental. In this case, it projects in the direction of the stimulus solely via the mind door.

So, if consciousness is so subtle, how do we cling to it? A person who is conscious of something can develop greed or clinging to consciousness by thinking, "I am so happy that I am conscious of this." A person can develop a certain sense of pride about his or her ability to become aware of certain things. For example, foodies are very proud of their awareness of subtle taste nuances.

Because we cling to the five aggregates, they keep us anchored in samsara, the perpetual round of existence. However, through the practice of mindfulness meditation it is possible to begin to see them clearly, to loosen our grip on them, and eventually to totally eliminate clinging to them and the suffering that clinging causes.

ME, MYSELF, AND MINE

This section discusses the aggregates of clinging in relation to notions of me, myself, and mine. The first erroneous notion, "this is mine," is craving (Pali *tanha*); the second, "this is me" or "I am this," is conceit (Pali *mana*);

and the third, "this is my self," is wrong view (Pali *ditthi*). It is with these concepts that the unenlightened mind views the aggregates.

In *The Discourse to Suradha*, the Venerable Suradha asks the Buddha how one should see things in order to rid the mind of the tendency to cling to the notions of me, myself, and mine. The Buddha responds that one should regard all forms, whether subtle or gross, near or far, present or future, with correct wisdom: "This is not mine, this I am not, this is not my self."[13] So, what is this correct wisdom? How do we practice this reflection?

First, it is obvious that we cannot control anything in life, not even our own bodies. We cannot order the body to remain young and healthy, and we cannot keep anything forever. This life is a loan, not a purchase. And we do not own any of it because its entire content is impermanent.

Similarly, whenever we think "I am," that "I am" is gone the very next second, changing, disappearing, and transforming into a new "I am." This all happens so fast that it is indescribable. If I were to tell you the same sentence over and over again a thousand times, it would be different every time I said it. Every syllable, every intonation of my voice would be slightly different. And while saying it, I would change, and so would you. In the *Suttanipata* we can find the following stanza that illustrates this point beautifully:

> Look at this world with its divine beings and humans. They are stuck in mentality and materiality. And they say, "this I am." While they are thinking, "I am," they are already changing. While they are thinking that this "I am" is true, the next moment it is not true. While they are thinking this "I am," it has changed. This is the truth. While they are thinking, "this I am," it becomes otherwise. So while they are thinking that this is true, it becomes a lie. But the noble ones do not think that this is "I."[14]

Thinking "this is 'I'" is the nature of confusion.

Similarly, the notion "this is my self" is wrong view. It is self-grasping. Interestingly enough, even the word *self* bears a connotation of grasping: it designates one's entity as separate from others and implies grasping at one's individualized personality. But because everything is in a constant state of flux, there really isn't anything to cling to. One who sees this with correct wisdom is freed from conceit. This profound teaching on impermanence is the key to liberation. If we really follow impermanence, the arising and falling of all phenomena, the mind lets go of clinging. And with the cessation of clinging, there comes the cessation of becoming into any state of existence. This is the end of suffering.

CHAPTER 2

Sankharas

WHAT ARE SANKHARAS?

SANKHARAS are intentional thoughts, words, and deeds triggered by the activation of underlying tendencies that are dormant in the mind. The first link of dependent origination presents the causal relationship between ignorance (the first step) and these sankharas (the second step). Due to its complexity, the meaning of the Pali word *sankhara* cannot be rendered into any modern language. It represents the coming into existence of any object (material or immaterial) or activity. Although all conditioned things are sankharas in the broadest sense of the term, in this particular teaching we are focusing on the dependent origination formula: when this arises, this arises. Therefore, we shall only consider them as dependently arising, conditioned things pertaining to our own mind-body complex.

What are these conditioned things? A thing that has come, is coming, or will come into existence is conditioned by factors that predetermine its nature. That thing in turn conditions other things. In short, everything is dependently arising; nothing can come into existence by itself. Anything that has arisen, is arising, or will arise depending on something else is a sankhara. An ordinary person accumulates countless sankharas throughout his or her life.

Sankharas therefore manifest in three stages—arising, mutation, and disappearance—that happen via causes and conditions, with the conditioned phenomenon conditioning what is coming into existence. This infinite dependency between previously occurring causal phenomena and their dependently arising outcome is the cycle and re-cycle of existence.

Let us further investigate this point using our knowledge of the physical body. Like the other aggregates, it exists and is already conditioned in a certain way. It is already formed, and we repair and maintain it every day. We take care of the body by consuming food, water, and air, providing it with shelter and clothing, using medicine, sleeping, waking up, working, exercising, and resting. The body is subject to being afflicted by all sorts of troubles: the elements, hunger and thirst, various diseases, and so on. Whatever the body is exposed to, whether something consumed or experienced through various circumstances, further conditions this conditioned body.

The breath, inhaling and exhaling, is one such body conditioner (Pali *kayasankhara*), and in fact pumping fresh air in and out of the body is the most essential one. It keeps us alive, the oxygen in our breath purifying our blood, which in turn circulates in the body in order to keep us alive. The conditioning of the other four aggregates (feelings, perceptions, thoughts, and consciousness) is likewise dependently arising. The conditional construction of the constituents that make up the mind-body complex is deterministic and based on the previous constructs.

Sankharas are active processes of constant preparing, adjusting, repairing, and re-adjusting. They are also extremely subtle. In one visible movement there are countless invisible transformations. At every moment, uncountable activities are going on inside our bodies and minds. In these subtle movements or activities, both mentality (contact, feeling, perception, thoughts, and attention) and materiality (the four elements of earth, water, fire, and air) merge in such a way that it is almost impossible for any such individual activity to be isolated and noticed.

The feelings that are triggered in our nerve fibers disappear just as quickly as they appear. We only notice the appearing and disappearing of the feelings we feel. These activities, along with perception, thoughts, attention, and consciousness, appear and disappear simultaneously. This simultaneous functioning is like one soup made up of many ingredients all blended together. With ignorance as a foundation, the boundaries between the arising, altering, and ceasing of the conditioned are blurred. All conditioned things are endowed with these characteristics of arising, altering, and passing away, which are in fact discernable. Therefore, it is possible to observe the constant, rapid changes that occur in sankharas.

Wisdom is the awareness of this rapid arising, altering, and passing away of everything that comes into existence through causes and conditions, which are sankharas. As wisdom arises, the mind becomes clear and the demarcation of boundaries between forms, feelings, perceptions, thoughts, and consciousness starts to appear. And these boundaries themselves are also arising, altering, and passing away constantly. They all appear and disappear every fraction of a second. With every heartbeat new forms, feelings, perceptions, thoughts, and consciousnesses arise and pass away.

SANKHARAS ARE CAMOUFLAGE

If we are not skillful enough our mind can make us believe that we are something we are not. Ignorance is very good at deceiving us that way, and if it is powerful enough we will not know that we are being deceived, making it even more difficult for us to escape from this deception. Sankharas, because they emerge from ignorance, have an intrinsically deceptive nature and camouflage themselves as friends. It is possible to spend our entire life deluded by our own mental formations, and even seemingly wholesome deeds are not always as they appear.

For instance, when you practice metta meditation, lust can appear as metta. Without being aware of this, you cultivate this lust and nourish it, all the while thinking that you are practicing metta. This is just like the parasites that live on some bodies and plants. Lust or romantic sentiments and metta can be mistaken for each other because they both concern the category of emotions of the heart. One can think that one is practicing metta while one's mind is truly gripped by romantic attachments. Hence, lust disguises itself as metta and acts like a parasite that robs the practitioner of the genuine feeling of metta.

In the same way, we nourish and hold on tightly to certain unwholesome thoughts. In Buddhist terminology, both wholesome and unwholesome thoughts are called dhammas. Lust is an unwholesome dhamma, while metta is a wholesome dhamma. When you practice wholesome thoughts without deep mindfulness, unwholesomeness sneaks into your mind as a friendly thought. Many practitioners who sincerely wish to practice wholesome dhammas succumb to unwholesome dhammas, unaware that this is happening due to the deceitful nature of sankharas. Deceptive dhammas keep us bound to sense pleasures.

For instance, our intention may be to give something, but the underlying tendencies of greed in our mind hinder our generosity. When we intend to give something, we also have unskillful desires and underlying tendencies. Good intention by itself is not enough; it must also be accompanied with wisdom. These intricacies demand our full, mindful attention in order for us to maintain a wholesome state of mind and act skillfully.

Sankharas can disguise themselves as wholesome while still being tainted by greed. Meditating and listening to the Dhamma are part of the collection of ten meritorious deeds, to be discussed further later in this chapter, but even attending meditation retreats can be prompted by underlying tendencies of greed and delusion. Some develop a superiority complex when they feel that their meditation practice and grasp of the Dhamma exceed that of others. This attitude of looking down on others hinders one's ability to conquer greed, hatred, and delusion. One thus acquires a deluded sense of spiritual progress.

There is no escape from sankharas. The Buddha explains that so long as we have a body, depending on our thinking or imagining, we commit sankharas due to underlying tendencies. Since they come into existence through causes and conditions they are dynamic, impermanent, in a constant state of flux. Not seeing this impermanence, the real nature of all conditioned things, we bring about suffering, disappointment, and dissatisfaction. The Buddha explains that whatever suffering arises, that suffering arises from sankharas.

As a term, *sankhara* implies the arising of the conditioned. They are triggered by the way we think, speak, or act. They recondition the conditioned body, feelings, perceptions, consciousness, and thoughts in order to deceive us. This is how ignorance causes reconditioning. And this is how sankharas arise, dependent on ignorance.

VOLITIONAL FORMATIONS

In *The Discourse on Being Devoured* the Buddha explains that sankharas are called volitional formations because they construct the conditioned.[15] The term *volition* means will, which is dependent on desire, which in turn arises based on ignorance. Supported by ignorance, a desire that has matured dependent on a certain condition further conditions the following sankhara. These volitional formations also construct the aggregates, with each aggregate being constructed based on its corresponding conditioned type. Volitional formations construct conditioned form as form, conditioned feeling as feeling, conditioned perception as perception, and so on.

The perception of the six sense-objects of forms, sounds, smells, tastes, tangibles, and mind-objects has a corresponding sixfold volition. After we perceive things connected to the five senses and the mind door, volition arises regarding those perceived objects. If the objects are perceived as pleasant and agreeable, craving arises for them. And if the objects are perceived as unpleasant and disagreeable, aversion arises for them. For this reason, craving arises through six channels: one for each type of sense-object. From this craving, volition regarding the objects of craving arises.

We have all experienced this. Suppose, for example, that you discover a kind of dessert that you have not tried before. Let's say it is delicious frozen custard from the famous Ted Drewes parlor in Saint Louis. Now the taste of the frozen custard is very pleasant, and even while you are consuming the creamy treat you tell yourself you really must come back there. There you have it! You have just conditioned yourself to develop an attachment to that dessert. But suppose the next time you walk by the store, it is closed. Now you are disappointed. Notice how disappointment arises from craving. The next day you see that the shop is open, and so you stand in the long line, eagerly awaiting your turn to place your order. So craving begets craving. The initial volitional formations that arose during your first visit to the frozen custard shop constructed the conditioning of your mind to return for another treat.

In this way volitional formations construct the conditioned. Our previous volitional formations, whether we committed them minutes, hours, days, or even years ago, have conditioned our current five aggregates: our body, feelings, perceptions, thoughts, and consciousness. And current volitional formations, from this moment on, condition our future five aggregates.

There is a sequence of steps leading from the first contact with the object through the sense and mind doors to mental proliferation. Based on contact, one feels; whatever one feels, one perceives; whatever one perceives, one thinks about; whatever one thinks about, one mentally proliferates. With mental proliferation as their source, perceptions and notions born of mental proliferation beset one with respect to past, future, and present forms cognizable through the senses and the mind.[16]

Volitional formations can be volitional activities that are wholesome, unwholesome, imperturbable, physical, verbal, or mental. Wholesome or unwholesome volitional activities using the body as an agent are called "physical volitional activities." Thoughts have to be formed in the mind before we talk; therefore applied and sustained thoughts are called "verbal volitional formations." Perception and feeling are mental activities and are thus called "mental volitional formations." Mental proliferations are the source of much stress and suffering in our lives. While wholesome mental proliferations, combined with mindfulness and concentration, can eventually lead us to liberation, unwholesome mental proliferations, combined with un-mindfulness and without concentration, result in endless suffering.

THE AGGREGATE OF SANKHARAS

Sankharas are collections of countless volitional thoughts, words, and deeds. These volitional formations, as their name implies, are made by will. As discussed in chapter 1, they are continuously renewed, conditioning and reconditioning us in this life and setting the stage for future lives. While volitional formations are one of the five aggregates, they also involve the five aggregates: in all activities where volition is involved, the five aggregates are present.

Let us explore how this works. Suppose that you decide to snap your fingers. When you do so, your two fingers are your body aggregate. Bringing them together and snapping them gives you feeling. With your eyes you can see what is happening. With your ears you can hear the sound of your snapping. When this happens the perception aggregate is involved. When you think about snapping your fingers the volitional formations aggregate is involved. You are aware of snapping your fingers, and so your consciousness aggregate is involved. For any volitional activity, whether in thought, speech, or deed, these five aggregates are involved.

Sankharas are thus intentional thoughts, words, and deeds that mold and shape the aggregates. They mold and modify our current aggregates, and they will mold and modify our future ones. How do intentional thoughts, words, and deeds do this? Suppose the thought of loving friendliness arises in your mind. Your mentality (contact, feeling, perception, thoughts, and attention) triggers the production of hormones and neurotransmitters responsible for enhancing positive feelings in the brain. The production of these feel-good hormones has many health benefits, including improved learning ability, regulation of motor functions, moods, appetite, and sleep patterns. You experience a deep sense of relaxation. Your mind and body are calm and serene. Your speech is gentle and friendly. Your deeds are peaceful. As a result, you generate more positive hormones in your brain, which makes you feel uplifted and peaceful. This positively affects your body, feelings, perceptions, thoughts, and consciousness.

On the other hand, if your thoughts happen to be charged with negativity such as hatred, jealousy, fear, or anxiety, then your mentality generates stress hormones. It is a well-known fact that stress causes a significant number of diseases and chronic health issues. Harboring negative thoughts can have a disastrous effect on the aggregates. Stress induced by negative thinking produces cortisol, which reduces the level of the serotonin neurotransmitter in the brain, and reduced serotonin levels are responsible for depression. The fight-or-flight bodily response resulting from negative thinking can also trigger severe and possibly life-threatening health issues and even alter the brain's neural pathways.

The Buddha stated that our intentional thoughts, words, and deeds condition our body, words, and mind. If mental sankharas are wholesome, the results are peaceful, delightful, calm, and happy, and if they are negative, the results are painful. We generate our joy and our misery by the way we think.

Here again, we find the explicit manifestation of the dependent origination formula in our daily lives. The health of our five aggregates depends on the quality of our accumulated thoughts. However, we generally lack the insight to see this within ourselves. We may read that negative thinking is bad for us in medical journals or news articles, but it doesn't click. This is because we lack the insight to understand the danger of negative thinking.

In this way negative mental volitional formations proliferate because they have been conditioned by previous negative mental volition. And they mature in our minds due to ignorance.

Wholesome, Unwholesome, and Imperturbable Sankharas

Thoughts are a form of action on the mental plane, nutriments that nourish our feelings. And since they produce pleasant feelings, they can be called sankharas. The collections of thoughts that constitute sankharas can be wholesome, unwholesome, and imperturbable. A collection of wholesome thoughts will produce pleasant feelings, while unwholesome thoughts will produce unpleasant feelings and imperturbable thoughts will produce equanimous feelings. Happiness is therefore synonymous with wholesome thoughts (and also wholesome words and deeds, of which thoughts are a precursor).

The content of our thoughts impacts our happiness; and the quality and content of our thoughts depend on our skill, our ability to cultivate wholesome thoughts. When we think unskillfully, the outcome of our thoughts doesn't make us happy no matter what we do—the manifestation of our thoughts on the physical, verbal, and mental planes are negative. But when we think skillfully, our thoughts make us joyous and our actions and speech are wholesome, resulting in a pleasant outcome.

There are three kinds of wholesome thoughts: thoughts of renunciation, of loving friendliness, and of compassion. Their opposites are the following three unwholesome thoughts: thoughts of greed, of hatred, and of cruelty. Imperturbable thoughts are generated when we attain higher states of absorption in meditation, or *jhana*s, to be discussed later in this chapter.

Thoughts are verbal conditioners because they condition the words we speak. We always have to think before speaking, for the thought process that precedes speech can be very quick, and we are rarely aware of the thinking that conditions our words. When greed for sensual pleasures invades the mind, the words conditioned by thoughts of sense pleasures express themselves as sensual desire. On the other hand, sensual thoughts

can be overcome by thoughts of letting go. Suppose that during meditation the thought of ice cream comes to your mind. You can overcome
it with a thought of letting go of that sensual thought about ice cream,
first by developing a thought of ice cream and then by talking yourself
into letting go of that thought. Your inner dialog is thus conditioned by
your thoughts, and your thoughts condition the words you say. Words
expressing kindness automatically produce thoughts of kindness in the
mind. The more we speak and think gentle thoughts, the more the mind
will be inclined toward kindness.

In the same way, thoughts of hatred, resentment, and anger are all
verbal conditioners with different strengths and nuances. An emotion such as anger, for instance, is a thought that conditions the words
we speak. When it arises it is an emotion that expresses itself in words,
either as internal dialog or as words outwardly spoken. The three types of
unwholesome word conditioners, such as these thoughts, are characterized by desire, aversion, and delusion, while the three kinds of wholesome
word conditioners are characterized by non-desire, non-aversion, and
non-delusion.

Because of ignorance we fail to see how such thoughts condition our
words, and we are therefore prone to letting unwholesome thoughts
arise and establish themselves in our minds. Right understanding of the
thought process that conditions our words is essential to overcome ignorance. In this process there is first the initial thought (Pali *vitakka*) and
then a subsequent sustained thought (Pali *vicara*). For instance, when
a thought of greed enters our mind and we continuously dwell on the
object of our greed by thinking and talking about how to accumulate
things, we enhance and maintain that thought of greed.

Due to ignorance we fail to see the drawbacks of harboring such
thoughts, but we can learn to cultivate the opposite of the unwholesome
initial thought by thinking about generosity, wisdom, and metta. With
correct understanding we see the danger in greed and cultivate thoughts
of its opposite, generosity, instead. Wisdom is the opposite of delusion,

and metta, or loving friendliness, is the opposite of anger, a wonderful state of mind that renders our speech gentle and uplifting. When we cultivate wholesome thoughts and sustain them repeatedly, they naturally condition our speech for the better. In the first two verses of the *Dhammapada*, the Buddha clearly states the importance of our state of mind when we act or speak:

> All experiences are preceded by mind,
> Led by mind,
> Made by mind.
> Speak or act with a corrupted mind,
> And suffering follows
> As the wagon wheel follows the hoof of the ox.
>
> All experiences are preceded by mind,
> Led by mind,
> Made by mind.
> Speak or act with a peaceful mind,
> And happiness follows
> Like a never-departing shadow.[17]

The mind governs whatever we do or say, and we must face the consequences of our words or deeds. Out of ignorance we commit wholesome, unwholesome, and imperturbable sankharas without knowing what we are doing. It is like groping in the dark. When we are in complete darkness we grasp onto anything that our hands contact. Such is craving—grasping in the dark. This combination of ignorance and craving working together brings forth the five aggregates of craving (see chapter 1).

THE CONNECTION BETWEEN KAMMA AND SANKHARAS

The wholesomeness or unwholesomeness of our sankharas has a direct effect on our kamma. Prompted by our underlying tendencies, we commit wholesome or unwholesome sankharas. The act we thus commit will bear fruit based on whether its nature is wholesome or unwholesome. That fruit is kamma, which follows the law of volitional causation. Volition, which is desire, is therefore an important part of the Buddhist understanding of kamma. Whenever we do anything intentionally and commit kamma, volition is there.

While the word *kamma* means "action," in Buddhism it also involves thinking. All thoughts, spoken words, and actions are always preceded by thinking. Therefore, it is thinking that makes an action kamma. Any wholesome or unwholesome action by body, speech, or mind that is committed intentionally with a mind gripped by greed, hatred, and delusion is kamma. But when the mind is free of greed, hatred, and delusion then our thoughts, words, and deeds are not kamma. The results of kamma depend on the intensity of greed, hatred, and delusion or that of non-greed, nonhatred, and nondelusion.

Committing kamma involves four stages: the underlying tendency stage, the arising stage, the movement in the direction of doing something (intent), and the actual stage of committing kamma. The wholesomeness or unwholesomeness of our kamma depends on our intention in the third stage. Let us consider the following scenario. Suppose that you got into an altercation with someone who initiated a physical attack and that you fatally injured your assailant in self-defense. You would be brought to criminal court for killing that person, and the verdict would most likely be "culpable homicide not amounting to murder." That means that you would not be punished for a capital offense. You may still be punished, but for a much lesser offense. Similarly, some minor effects of kamma may remain when intention is not there, but these do not constitute major kamma.

Accompanying intention in the mind are contact, feeling, and thought. Consciousness is present in all these and is the component that activates the factors of contact, feeling, perception, and volitional formations. When we feel, perceive, think, or pay attention, consciousness is active. Without it, there would be no awareness of the mentality factors.

For this reason, consciousness is referred to as a seed, and as the seed of consciousness grows it is nourished by the water of greed. Without greed, consciousness and the other mentality factors don't work together to sprout and create kamma. Thought, intention, deliberation, and the underlying tendencies become the field in which consciousness grows. Even without intention and deliberation, as long as underlying tendencies remain consciousness will take root. But if there are no intentions, deliberations, or underlying tendencies, then consciousness cannot take root, grow, and produce results. This is why the Buddha said, "When one thinks, and deliberates, or has underlying tendencies, this becomes the foundation for consciousness to hold on."[18]

The domain in which kamma (whether sensual kamma, kamma with form, or formless kamma) ripens corresponds to the domain in which its maturation can be discerned. For example, kamma based on greed produces a painful result when that greed bears fruit. If you are greedy for food, your kamma may fructify as indigestion. It is a sensual kamma that bears fruit in the sensual domain. To know this effect, you must be aware of it. You discern the maturation of this kamma in the same domain where you planted the seed, the intention for taste pleasure. Kamma is the field. It provides the medium for the discernment (seed) of its fruit. The seed is consciousness. It becomes established and takes root in a particular domain when it is nourished by craving.

Due to ignorance, fed by underlying tendencies, mental cogitation and deliberation proliferate. Thus, dependent on ignorance, volitional formations arise, the first step of dependent origination.

KAMMA IS NOT FATALISM

We commit kamma every day by body, speech, and mind—in theory, practice, and result. It is sometimes referred to as the law of causality.

While it is true that the intensity of the outcome of kamma depends on intention, it is not possible to determine its exact fruition. Kamma does not involve equal and opposite forces like a classical mechanics problem for a system in equilibrium. For instance, if you hit someone with an impact of fifty newtons, the fruition of your kamma is unlikely to be that you get hit back with an impact of fifty newtons. This is physically improbable, and the fruition of kamma depends on many other factors beside the act itself.

Kamma is quite complex and can easily be misunderstood, as the following story from *The Discourse on the Great Exposition of Kamma* illustrates. The wanderer Potaliputta told the Venerable Samiddhi, a disciple of the Buddha, that he had heard the Buddha saying, "Bodily action is vain, verbal action is vain, only mental action is real," and "There is that attainment on entering which one does not feel anything at all." The Venerable Samiddhi disagreed with this statement, saying, "Having done an intentional action by way of body, speech, or mind, one feels suffering [as its result], friend Potaliputta."

Upon hearing of this conversation, the Buddha corrected the Venerable Samiddhi's statement: "Having done an intentional action by way of body, speech, and mind [whose result is] to be felt as pleasant, one feels pleasure. Having done an intentional action by way of body, speech, and mind [whose result is] to be felt as painful, one feels pain. Having done an intentional action by way of body, speech, and mind [whose result is] to be felt as neither-pain-nor-pleasure, he feels neither-pain-nor-pleasure."[19]

A partial understanding of kamma leads to dogma, a rigid, linear view of kamma as a one-to-one correspondence between kammic deeds and rebirth conditions. Thinking that a good person always comes to a happy rebirth and that an evildoer always experiences hellish conditions in the next life is too simplistic. Some kamma produces immediate results while other kamma continues over several lifetimes.

We find an illustration of such an erroneous and fatalistic understanding of kamma in *The Discourse on the Horn Blower*.[20] In this discourse the

Buddha asks Asibandhakaputta, a disciple of Mahavira, the leader of the Jains, what his teacher instructs his followers. Mahavira's teaching, says Asibandhakaputta, is that rebirth is entirely determined by the actions one has undertaken in life, that everyone who kills living beings, steals, commits sexual misconduct, or lies goes to a place of deprivation, a woeful plane of existence after death. The Buddha is quick to point out the flaw in that logic, asking Asibandhakaputta if the amount of time one takes to commit a particular wrong deed such as killing is greater than the overall duration of time one takes not engaging in such activities throughout one's life. Since a crime is an isolated event of normally short duration, obviously the answer to this question is no. This implies that according to Mahavira's reasoning, no one would go to a woeful destination after death. Mahavira's error is that he holds an extreme and fatalistic view of kamma. What hope for liberation remains for his disciples, who, being misled, act unskillfully?

While the Buddha criticized wrong deeds and taught his disciples to refrain from them, his disciples learned to reflect wisely on their acts. This wise reflection led them to abandon unwholesome actions and thoughts and to cultivate a boundless heart filled with loving friendliness. Having trained their minds thus, the Buddha's disciples overcame greed, hatred, and delusion.

It is also essential to understand that one should not constantly reminisce about wrong kamma done in the past, as this is counterproductive for liberation from suffering. If a generally virtuous person, having committed unwholesome kamma once, were to dwell on it constantly, this thought would enter their mind at the moment of death and negatively impact their next rebirth. On the other hand it is beneficial to remember the good things that we have done in life. This makes us happy and motivates us to continue doing good.

Of course, when we do something good we may not always find an opportunity to repeat it, but we can nevertheless think about it every day and at all times. As a result the mind becomes happy and relaxed and thus geared toward what is wholesome. It is just like a jug filled with pure water drop by drop; eventually it gets filled to the brim. Similarly, thinking of wholesome things again and again increases our wholesomeness. Beautiful verses from the *Dhammapada* emphasize the workings of kamma and the attitude one should adopt to live a wholesome and virtuous life:

> Be quick to do good,
> Restrain your mind from evil.
> When one is slow to make merit,
> One's mind delights in evil.

> Having done something evil,
> Don't repeat it,
> Don't wish for it:
> Evil piled up brings suffering.

> Having done something meritorious,
> Repeat it,
> Wish for it:
> Merit piled up brings happiness.

> Even an evildoer may see benefit
> As long as the evil
> Has yet to mature.
> But when the evil has matured,
> The evildoer
> Will meet with misfortune.

> A doer of good may meet evil fortune
> As long as the good
> Has yet to mature.
> But when the good has matured,

The doer of good
Will meet with good fortune.

Don't disregard evil, thinking,
"It won't come back to me!"
With dripping drops of water
Even a water jug is filled.
Little by little,
A fool is filled with evil.

Don't disregard merit, thinking,
"It won't come back to me!"
With dripping drops of water
Even a water jug is filled.
Little by little,
A sage is filled with merit.[21]

Therefore, kamma is not fatalism. It is a factor that has come to fruition and is bearing results. But it is not, however, a purely physical cause-
and-effect phenomenon. It involves thoughts; without thoughts, we
cannot make kamma. Kamma is also neither pessimistic nor optimistic;
it's the way that things happen. It is our inheritance, our property, our
relation. We are the result of our kamma. Whatever kamma we commit,
wholesome or unwholesome, we are its owners; we are totally responsible
for what we think, say, and do. We cannot pass the buck to somebody else
and say, "It is not my responsibility. I did not do this. So and so started
it," and so on. When we commit an action we must be psychologically
and physically strong enough to be honest and sincere in accepting our
responsibility. This is a very practical teaching in taking responsibility.

FOUR CATEGORIES OF KAMMA

In the Pali tradition kamma comes in various categories according to their results. Wholesome deeds produce wholesome results and unwholesome deeds produce unwholesome results. *Punna*, or "wholesome," kamma constitutes a collection of wholesome activities leading to accumulated good results that lead to an enjoyable samsaric existence. They bring happiness and stand in opposition to *apunna* kamma, which constitutes unwholesome activities whose fruit will ripen to yield painful outcomes. Note that even neutral activities (imperturbable, neither wholesome nor unwholesome) are kamma if their basis lies in greed and ignorance. Both punna and apunna kamma keep a person trapped in the endless cycle of samsara since both contain the underlying tendency of greed.

One can do something very wholesome and meritorious, but if one has an ulterior motive such as a desire for recognition, an attachment to being praised for one's actions, it is punna kamma. Any act done out of greed, hatred, and delusion, no matter how noble it may be, has its basis in ignorance and thus maintains the endless cycle of rebirth. The disastrous consequences of apunna kammas are more obvious: when we do wrong by body, speech, or mind, suffering inevitably arises.

Kusala, or "skillful," kamma is called the quality controller of punna kamma. It consists of mental, verbal, and physical activities done without any trace of greed, hatred, and delusion. We act without expecting anything in return, and our motive is the complete removal of the hindrances in order to attain liberation. If greed, hatred, and delusion arise during a wholesome act, kusala kamma intervenes and removes them from the mind. For example, suppose that you are working on a generous and wholesome project and suddenly anger arises in your mind. With proper practice, kusala kamma can intervene and remove that anger, along with greed and delusion.

Just as apunna is the opposite of punna, *akusala* is the opposite of kusala, with akusala kamma being unskillful thoughts, words, and deeds that support apunna kamma. While punna, apunna, and akusala kamma keep us in samsara and prolong our woeful and painful existence, kusala kamma is a kamma that removes hindrances on the way to liberation from samsara.

Five factors contribute to a kamma coming to fruition. First, there must be a recipient of the kamma. In the case of killing, that would be a living being. To continue this example, the second would be that one must know that it is a living being. The third factor is intention, and the fourth is the method employed to carry out the deed. The fifth is the completion of the kamma using the intended method. When all these factors are present the kamma is complete. An incomplete kamma does not have the power to generate the full results, as in the earlier example of killing an assailant in self-defense. In the case of the wholesome kamma of generosity, the five factors would be (1) a recipient of a gift, (2) knowing that there is a recipient, (3) the intention to give, (4) the material for the donation and method of giving, and (5) the delivery of the gift.

Kamma has effects that manifest in this life and the next; the kamma that occurs close to death precipitates the next life. Upon rebirth kamma manifests as habitual kamma, accumulated (residual) kamma, and heavy kamma. Each of these can also be characterized as (un)wholesome or (un)skillful, and we will explore each of these three below.

Habitual kamma is what we do on a regular basis. In the absence of heavy kamma, habitual kamma determines our next rebirth. Accumulated kamma is the sum of residual kamma from the past and also contributes to the conditions of our next life. While habitual and accumulated kamma tend to produce immediate results, heavy kamma becomes prominent in the mind at the time of death. Therefore, heavy kamma becomes the dominant factor defining the circumstances and conditions of our next rebirth.

Five heavy kammas are regarded as particularly unwholesome: (1) killing one's mother, (2) killing one's father, (3) killing an arahant, (4) hurting a buddha with malicious intent, and (5) creating a schism in the Sangha.

However, a key factor is that a negative kamma is only heavy if it is done with malicious intent. For example, when the Buddha's personal physician Jivaka performed surgery on the Buddha's foot to remove a splinter, he had to cut the wound open to clean it.[22] In this case there was no malicious intention of causing the Buddha pain, and so the surgery did not entail heavy unwholesome kamma.

Wholesome heavy kammas, on the other hand, include the following:

- generosity;
- morality;
- attaining the eight degrees of jhana (meditative absorption);
- reverence for the Buddha, Dhamma, and Sangha;
- service to others, attending to one's duties with care;
- sharing merit;
- rejoicing in the merit of others;
- listening to the Dhamma;
- teaching the Dhamma; and
- straightening one's views.

Let us elaborate, for example, on the benefit of practicing the jhanas in making wholesome kamma. The higher the degree of jhana, the greater the benefit. When one attains the first and second jhanas, one takes rebirth in fine material spheres, where lifetimes are extremely long and existence is very refined. When one attains the third and fourth jhanas, one takes rebirth in even finer realms, culminating in the highest realm of the pure abodes. One of four outcomes can occur upon attaining the fourth jhana: (1) one can be born on a higher plane called the Brahma realm; (2) one can develop various miraculous powers; (3) one can gain vision and knowledge (the realization of the path leading to liberation); and (4) one destroys the remaining influxes (asavas). The next four meditative absorptions are the immaterial jhanas, the highest degree of which is attaining the cessation of perception and feeling. Having attained this jhana, one takes rebirth in the plane of neither-perception-nornonperception, the subtlest of the immaterial spheres. In these higher realms, kamma is called imperturbable because once that state is attained one can maintain it for seven days. To attain that state, greed and anger must be overcome.

WHOLESOME AND UNWHOLESOME KAMMA

Kammas are sankharas done with intention. As discussed in the previous section, the intention to commit actions by body, speech, or mind can be imbued with wholesome or unwholesome tendencies. Kamma committed with underlying tendencies of greed, hatred, and delusion is unwholesome, while kamma devoid of those unskillful roots is wholesome. An ignorant person has only a partial understanding of the unwholesome, the wholesome, and their roots. As a result, this person would be subject to rebirth even though they may have done a great many good deeds in their lifetime. Since all actions that we undertake are physical, verbal, and mental, so too are kammas; traditionally this is broken down into a wholesome set of three physical, four verbal, and three mental kammas and a corresponding unwholesome set. Each will be explored below.

The three unwholesome physical types of kammas are killing, stealing, and sensual misconduct. Killing, no matter its intent, is done in ignorance. We may try to justify it in many ways, but ignorance always underlies any act of killing. Those who kill may not like to hear that it is done in ignorance; they may think their action will benefit some. But with enough wisdom, we can find another way of helping others. Without the wisdom and insight to find another way that does not require taking a life, we remain in ignorance.

Stealing can be falsely appropriating material things, but it can also apply to immaterial things such as ideas, time, energy, and so on. Many things can be stolen under the premise of all kinds of justifications and excuses. Sometimes, people even steal Buddha statues and meditation cushions. Taking something like a statue of the Buddha under the pretext that the Buddha does not belong to anybody in particular and that the statue is therefore free to be taken from a monastery is wrong. The statue means a lot to those attending the monastery, and they revere it with great faith. Therefore, losing this sacred object is a cause for great sadness for them, even if the statue is tiny. And so, no matter how tiny the stolen item, stealing causes harm.

The next bodily unskillful kamma is sensual misconduct. Note that we are saying *sensual* instead of *sexual*, and the distinction is meaningful. Sensual misconduct means abusing our eyes, ears, nose, tongue, body, and mind. And how do we abuse them?

Our eyes are exposed to whatever we look at all day long, and we often intentionally expose our eyes to things that pollute our minds. Some people keep watching various things on television or on the internet or read things that pollute the mind. This form of misconduct through sight is abusing the eyes. In the same way, we have misconduct related to hearing. Some enjoy listening to gossip and unpleasant things said about others, and some like to join this kind of unwholesome conversation. By doing so, they unknowingly commit unwholesome kamma. The unwholesome will never produce anything wholesome but will surely yield unwholesome results. When we plant bitter gourd seeds, we certainly cannot expect to reap apples from this crop. The result will be bitter. Along the same vein, we abuse the nose and tongue. I have heard that children who are addicted to illicit drugs sometimes go to the hardware store in order to sniff paint thinners or magic markers to get high. This is how we abuse our nose. We abuse our tongue when we eat the wrong kind of food or when we eat too much. Although the food seems very tasty when consumed, later on it produces unwholesome results. We abuse our body through sexual misconduct, and this too produces unwholesome and painful results. Finally, there is abuse of the mind. We abuse our mind by not using it through idleness, by not cultivating it properly, and by letting it be bombarded with unwholesome mental states.

The four unwholesome verbal kammas are related to wrong speech: telling lies, slanderous talk, talk that is imbued with hatred, and gossip. Telling lies has the potential to break friendships. Slanderous or malicious speech can cause people who habitually look at each other with friendly eyes to develop unfriendly feelings toward one another. A longstanding friendship can be destroyed by such speech. This is very harmful, unwholesome kamma. Harsh, accusing speech, whether direct or indirect, is likewise an unskillful use of language. Using speech just to kill time or gossip is a totally useless kind of speech, another unskillful use of words. Behind all these different kinds of unskillful speech lies ignorance of the harmful nature of such words.

Now that we've discussed physical and verbal unwholesome kamma, we come to the three unwholesome mental kammas: covetousness, hatred, and having wrong view. Intense greed or covetousness belongs in this category; greed for someone else's property—that is, the desire to acquire it for oneself—can become strong enough to push someone to steal. Other forms of mental kammas with disastrous consequences are hatred, anger, and vengefulness. These are all intensely negative mental states that cause other beings much suffering. Finally we have wrong view. As discussed earlier, wrong view is far more dangerous than poison in the sense that it can cause harm to oneself and destroy one's future in this life and the next, keeping us in the endless cycle of samsara.

On the wholesome side, the three physical kammas are abstaining from killing, abstaining from stealing, and abstaining from sensual misconduct. In this context, abstaining involves more than just restraint and includes a positive movement as well. For instance, abstaining from killing involves not taking lives and going even further by improving and supporting life to the extent possible. Similarly, abstaining from stealing also implies protecting others by thoughts, words, and deeds by ensuring that their property and lives are safe. Abstaining from sensual misconduct involves restraint over the senses. We abuse our senses by overindulging in them. The same goes for the mind when we allow ourselves to get lost in sensual thought. This lack of restraint on the part of the six senses (the sixth being the mind) increases greed, hatred, and delusion and keeps us bound in samsara. On the other hand, skillful use of our eyes, ears, nose, tongue, body, and mind reduces greed, hatred, and delusion.

Wholesome speech restraint is fourfold. First, one should be truthful and refrain from telling lies. One should not engage in slanderous talk that harms others. One's speech should be cordial and friendly and not filled with harsh words. Finally, one should not engage in useless idle chatter and instead discuss something meaningful and uplifting. Ideally, one should discuss Dhamma whenever possible. One may argue that in our day-to-day lives—at work, for instance—we cannot discuss the Dhamma. But even in these circumstances, our speech can be filled with the wisdom of the Dhamma. We can discuss how to do our job better, more efficiently, and with more concentration. We can foster a supportive and uplifting atmosphere at our workplace and discuss many job-related topics without gossiping.

Regarding the three wholesome mental kammas, we can overcome greed by practicing generosity. Instead of being covetousness, one should take up the practice of giving without any reservation, distinction, or discrimination. One should give freely to anyone, including animals. We can replace anger with the practice of loving friendliness, a very wholesome and meritorious deed with great benefits. Finally, wrong view must be overcome with right understanding, which is foremost in removing ignorance.

CHAPTER 3

Consciousness

WHAT IS CONSCIOUSNESS?

CONSCIOUSNESS MEANS awareness, and it is our most vital force. While it is not something tangible that can be directly observed, we all know we have it. When someone becomes unconscious, we try to do various things to revive them, but we don't know where their consciousness went. It hides when the nervous system is paralyzed or in deep sleep when it becomes dormant or inactive.

Where does it come from? In *The Discourse on the Honeyball*, the Buddha has this to say on the matter:

> Dependent on the eye and forms, eye-consciousness arises. The meeting of the three is contact. With contact as condition there is feeling. What one feels, that one perceives. What one perceives, that one thinks about. What one thinks about, that one mentally proliferates. With what one has mentally proliferated as the source, perceptions and notions [born of] mental proliferation beset a man with respect to past, future, and present forms cognizable through the eye.[23]

To become active, in other words, consciousness needs an object to be conscious of. When the senses make contact with an object, awareness of the object through the senses is required in order to recognize it. When we are asleep, for instance, a sound that is loud enough wakes us up. We become conscious of the sound. This awareness of an object in relation to the senses and the mind is called eye-, ear-, nose-, tongue-, body-, and mind-consciousness, respectively.

When the mind is active, consciousness projects in the direction of the sense and mind doors. When they are closed or when we are in deep sleep or are unconscious, the mind becomes conscious of itself since it can then only reflect itself. When we regain our senses and the nervous system is again fully active, consciousness wakes up and an outside trigger is perceived through the sense doors. Consciousness has, therefore, a waking and an activation phase so that when it finds a door, it raises its head and goes through that door. Once it has become activated, we begin to act in a wholesome or unwholesome way based on our particular state of mind at that time.

Take the word *space*, for instance. As soon as we hear the word, an image arises in our mind, and we become conscious of that image. First the sound contacts our ears, then sensory feeling associated with hearing arises. At that time, we perceive the word *space* and recognize its meaning. The thought of space then enters our minds. At each stage, consciousness must be present. The meeting of the senses, sense-objects, and consciousness is called *contact*. Once contact is established, feeling arises, and the sequence of steps from feeling to thinking takes place.

Hence, there is no arising of consciousness independent of form, contact, feeling, perception, mental activities, and consciousness—that is, outside of the five aggregates. Consciousness, therefore, is not an isolated and self-contained entity that continues from life to life.

Consciousness is Dependently Arising

In *The Discourse on the Destruction of Craving* we read about a monk who held on to a wrong view of consciousness as a separate, permanent entity.[24] As related to us in this sutta, the Venerable Sati had developed the pernicious view that it is the same consciousness that on one hand feels and experiences the results of actions performed and on the other goes through the rounds of death and rebirth in samsara. The Buddha reprimanded him for this erroneous understanding of consciousness and explained that without a condition, consciousness cannot arise. Depending on sense-objects as conditions, consciousness arises through the senses, just like a fire burns based on the kind of material that fuels it. And when the causes of its arising cease, consciousness also ceases, just like a fire goes out when its fuel is used up.

In many ways consciousness is like a magic show. Magicians are masters of illusions; their tricks make us think that we are seeing something that isn't actually there. They create the illusion of something that does not exist now and will not exist in the future. Similarly, consciousness is invisible, untouchable, constantly in motion, and changing at every instant. It arises whenever sankharas—constantly changing activities—take place. Whenever something happens, consciousness immediately identifies the source of the activity and starts to investigate. Consciousness arises at the same speed as the phenomenon that triggered it. In fact, it changes so rapidly, faster than anything else we could imagine, that it passes away as a different consciousness from the one it arose as. The Buddha said that he could not even find a simile for the speed at which consciousness changes. Consciousness is perpetually arising and falling, arising again and disappearing. To refine this further, it is not a thing that falls or disappears at all. Rather, it is the arising that disappears. Thus, the ever-fleeting consciousness is in a constant state of flux or oscillation.

The belief in consciousness as an autonomous and permanent entity stems from ignorance and craving. What Venerable Sati failed to grasp is that consciousness, which has arisen, cannot remain without an awareness of something. Therefore, consciousness arises dependent on sankharas (the second step of dependent origination) and ceases with their ending.

Mental activities and consciousness are interconnected. The mind has three main functions: thinking, the ability to create, and the capacity to become aware of what is created, what is being thought about, and what is happening. These three functions cannot be separated, as they are intrinsically connected. Together, they are called *consciousness*. Consciousness is never isolated and is always identified with something else. For instance, there is consciousness with or without greed, with or without hatred, and with or without delusion. It always arises with mental factors, which cannot exist without it.

Once contact is established based on consciousness, feeling arises and sustained attention leads to mental proliferation. In *The Discourse on the Greater Set of Questions and Answers*, an exchange between the Venerable Sariputta and the Venerable Maha Kotthita sheds light on this connection between the mentality factors of feeling, perception, and consciousness.[25] The Venerable Maha Kotthita asks, "Feeling, perception, and consciousness, friend—are these states conjoined or disjoined? And is it possible to separate each of these states from the others in order to describe the difference between them?" And the Venerable Sariputta responds:

> Feeling, perception, and consciousness, friend—these states are conjoined, not disjoined, and it is impossible to separate each of these states from the others in order to describe the difference between them. For what one feels, that one perceives; and what one perceives, that one cognizes. That is why these states are conjoined, not disjoined, and it is impossible to separate each of these states from the others in order to describe the difference between them.

Consciousness is the constituent that underlies all the mentality factors. And consciousness itself cannot exist without consciousness. Knowledge of form (materiality), for example, is based on designating characteristics and requires consciousness. The relationship between consciousness and mentality and materiality is like two bamboo sticks that support each other and join at the top. When the consciousness bamboo falls, so does the mentality and materiality stick. Consciousness keeps going back and forth like a pendulum between mentality and materiality. And consciousness becomes conscious of itself by being aware of the subtlest states of mentality and materiality. That is why consciousness is present even when the senses are not functioning.

In life consciousness and mentality and materiality always coexist. Their mutual dependency begins at the time of conception; if consciousness is not there at conception, mentality and materiality do not grow, for they have no support. And if consciousness departs the mother's womb, mentality and materiality cannot continue to remain and the embryo will not grow. Therefore, mentality and materiality arise dependent on consciousness, the third step of dependent origination.

The Nutriment of Consciousness

Consciousness is constantly bombarded by sensory perceptions. The Buddha illustrated this fact with the simile of a king punishing a bandit over and over again. In this story, the bandit receives one hundred lashes in the morning, another hundred at noon after surviving that ordeal, and yet another hundred in the evening. But the bandit is so resilient that he survives this repeated abuse. Our consciousness is similarly impinged upon by our minds and senses. Just think about the countless things that we have seen, heard, smelled, tasted, touched, and thought about throughout our lives! All of these impinged on our consciousness.

The Buddha describes the role of consciousness in our mind-body complex using the following simile. Suppose that there is a city protected by six gates. Messengers enter through these gates and ask the gatekeepers where the lord of the city resides. The gatekeepers reply that the lord resides at the crossroad at the center of the city, then the messengers deliver their message and exit through these same doors.

These gates are the six senses. Consciousness is the lord, sitting at the center of the city, who receives all sorts of messages from the senses, including stress, anger, greed, resentment, pain, and suffering. Everything brought in through the mind and sense doors goes through consciousness. So we can say that, like the bandit in the first story, it receives lashes morning, noon, and night. And just as the bandit did not succumb to repeated blows, consciousness persists, though gripped by greed, hatred, and delusion. It is always present and in motion, constantly vacillating between mentality and materiality. Only once the mind is completely freed from all defilements is it able to remain equanimous, no matter what comes through our six senses.

We have no control over consciousness: it spontaneously arises whenever sensory or mental objects come through our six senses. Whenever our eyes come into contact with a visual object, eye-consciousness arises. Provided that our optics are functioning properly and we are awake and conscious, there is no way to prevent this, as it occurs naturally and spontaneously. Similarly, as soon as we think, consciousness arises. There is no way to escape consciousness.

As soon as sense, sense-object, and consciousness meet, contact arises. Contact in turn conditions feeling. Feeling conditions craving, which leads to clinging, becoming, rebirth, and this entire mass of suffering. In this way consciousness becomes a nutriment that supports and sustains future existence.

In Pali, a nutriment is called *ahara*, meaning "that which is brought in." Having heard that consciousness is such a nutriment, the Venerable Moliya-Phagguna once asked the Buddha the following question: "Venerable Sir, who consumes the nutriment of consciousness?" The Buddha corrected him, saying, "Phagguna, that is not a valid question.... If you had asked me what conditions the nutriment of consciousness, that would be a valid question."[26] The pronoun *who* implies a person, whereas *what* designates a phenomenon. This phenomenon is that which is conditioned by the senses and becomes the seed (i.e., nutriment) for future existence. The chain of conditionality, starting from the conjunction of the senses, sense-object, and consciousness that gives rise to contact, goes all the way to rebirth.

The arising of craving causes the arising of the nutriment of consciousness. The sustenance of life depends on food. We consume physical food to sustain the body out of a desire to maintain it, and we consume physical and mental food (contact, volitional formations, and consciousness) to sustain the five aggregates, which, when sustained by desire, are called the five aggregates of clinging or suffering. Craving, nutriments, the five aggregates, and suffering are all interconnected. And with the cessation of craving comes the cessation of nutriments, the five aggregates, and suffering.

The constantly changing nature of consciousness yields its power. Seeing changes in the body and deducing its impermanent nature is easy. We generally do not see the changes as they occur, but we can observe what has changed over time. Wrinkles, grey hair, and saggy muscles start to appear as the years go by. But changes in consciousness are much more elusive to grasp, as they occur at a much faster rate than bodily changes. If something oscillates very quickly, it looks like it is not changing at all, because we usually cannot perceive anything above a specific frequency. It is just like that for consciousness, and as a result we tend to view consciousness as something permanent, something belonging to us, a "me." It is only when practicing mindful meditation, which gives insight into the vibratory makeup of consciousness, that its nature can be objectively observed. With this proper insight, letting go of the erroneous view of consciousness as self is indeed possible.

REBIRTH CONSCIOUSNESS

Rebirth occurs by means of mental force, which is present in consciousness. Kamma, ignorance, and desire give rise to the will to exist, and these four phenomena arise in conjunction for rebirth to occur.

At the moment of death this mental force, kamma, ignorance, and desire come together. The mental force occurring at the last moment of consciousness becomes the seed in the field of kamma. When you commit kamma, then and there the kamma is finished. But this constantly changing, impermanent consciousness has the seed of what a person has done throughout their entire life, and in that consciousness is also kamma. Without consciousness you cannot commit kamma, because thought, the prerequisite of kamma, does not arise without consciousness.

At the actual moment of death this consciousness, together with the mental force, leaves the body. At that time there arises in the dying person's mind a vision of where they are going to be born according to their kamma. Even if it is a very miserable place, at that moment their consciousness creates a beautiful picture. If they are going to be reborn in a hellish state at the time of death, this will look most pleasant to their mind. And so rebirth happens according to their state of mind. If it is gripped with desire and ignorance, the kammic force combined with consciousness contains the seed of the good and the bad that the person has done throughout their life. This happens instantaneously at the moment of death. As we read in the *Dhammapada*, one who dies will be cut off from life, leave this existence instantly, and take rebirth in the place where they are going to be reborn:

> You are now at the end of life;
> You're headed for Yama's presence
> With no resting place along the way,
> No provision for the journey.
> Make an island for yourself.
> Be quick in making effort. Be wise.
> Unblemished, with corruption removed,
> You'll experience birth and old age no more.[27]

CHAPTER 4

Mentality and Materiality

THE PALI TERM for mentality and materiality is *nama-rupa*, with *nama* meaning "name," and *rupa*, "form." Name is pervasive; it is the label we put on things whenever we think about them. We use names and labels to understand physical and mental objects. The meaning of the object is associated with its name.

This is reminiscent of the story of the Venerable Anuruddha, a prominent monk at the time of the Buddha, who was very spoiled as a child. His mother never refused him anything, and he always got whatever he wanted. He had a boy assistant who fetched anything he asked for. One day Anuruddha asked this boy to bring him some cake from the royal household. But on that day Anuruddha's mother regrettably told the attendant boy that the kitchen had run out and there was no cake. Since Anuruddha had never been refused anything in his life, he did not know the meaning of the word *no* and told his attendant, "Well, then bring me 'no cake.'"

The attendant returned to the royal household and told Anuruddha's mother that her son had asked for no cake. So the confused mother gave him an empty bowl covered with a lid to bring to her son. But when Anuruddha opened the top, he saw a cake in the bowl. It was later said that Anuruddha had done so many meritorious deeds in his previous lives that he had won the graces of the deities, who filled the bowl with the most delicious cake that anyone could ever have tasted. And from that time on Anuruddha always asked his mother for "no cake."

This story illustrates how names or labels are that which give meaning to things. They are, in fact, conventions that we use to represent and define things. Our calendar is divided into months, weeks, and days. This is commonly accepted; no one has ever touched or felt Saturday, but it represents a particular day based on our social constructs. Anything we can think of has a name. Even abstract concepts can only be pondered through the name that they are given.

In dependent origination, names take on a broader meaning in that they constitute the group called *mentality*. In general names refer not to the mind but to objects in the material world, but in our study of dependent origination our focus is entirely on mental states. To describe our subjective feelings and communicate our mental states, we use names. And in order to recognize and identify the feelings described by these names, consciousness must be active since the mentality and materiality factors depend on consciousness. Therefore, the term *mentality*, which encompasses mental states, is better suited than *name* to the subject at hand, which is the understanding of the law of repetition and dependency inherent within dependent origination.

When we described the consciousness aspect of dependent origination in the previous chapter, we introduced the factors of mentality and materiality, between which consciousness oscillates. Mentality consists of contact, feeling, perception, thought, and attention. All of these factors are related to the mind, and each one performs a specific function in dependent origination.

Contact—the meeting of the six senses, the corresponding sense-objects, and consciousness—yields feeling. And in order to become aware of feelings, consciousness must be present. Therefore, feelings depend on contact and consciousness. They also belong to the domain of the mind, as they cannot be seen, heard, touched, smelled, or tasted. Similarly, perception, thoughts, and attention are purely mental factors.

We experience the world through the materiality factors composed of the four great elements: air, water, earth, and fire. But what we experience by means of these elements is through feelings. The earth element exhibits the property of hardness, which is something that can be felt rather than seen. When you touch something hard and press against it, you feel stiffness. The water element exhibits the property of binding. The composition of the H_2O molecule is such that the oxygen atom in one water molecule is electrostatically attracted to one of the hydrogen atoms in a nearby water molecule. This leads to the binding property of water molecules to each other called *cohesion*, while adhesion is the binding property of water to other substances. The fire element exhibits the property of heat, the air element that of movement. We get an impression of the properties of hardness or softness, binding, heat, and movement from the elements that make up the materiality factor.

Also included in mentality and materiality are our five physical senses along with the mind, collectively referred to as the sixfold sense base. Without mentality and materiality, the six senses cannot exist. This brings us to the fourth step of dependent origination: dependent on mentality and materiality, the sixfold base arises. We will explore this further in the next chapter.

CHAPTER 5

The Sixfold Base

ONTACT, the first mentality factor, is the meeting of the senses, sense-objects, and sense-consciousness. The five physical senses and the mind constitute the sixfold sense base and are the foundation upon which contact occurs. When the contact mentality factor arises, it does so through the eyes, ears, nose, tongue, body, and mind. Consciousness, meanwhile, is the vital energy that allows the senses to operate and provides awareness of the experience occurring through the sense and mind doors. As soon as eye-, ear-, nose-, tongue-, body-, and mind-consciousness arise, so does the sixfold sense base. When the sixfold sense base is impinged upon, the consciousness corresponding to the triggered sense arises.

Consciousness and the sixfold sense base are thus mutually supporting factors. In fact, the Pali word for sense base, *alayatana*, means "that wherein consciousness operates," and without consciousness, the sixfold base cannot function. It is the simultaneous arising of consciousness along with the bases that allows the senses to operate.

Once contact is established, perception of the sense-object occurs based on the name associated with the form, which is characterized by materiality factors. For instance, when you taste milk, your taste buds contact milk, and you become conscious of the taste of milk. You don't call it *butter*; you call it *milk*. That is the label put on the substance that you recognize and identify as milk. Without a name or the ability to create a name, there could be no perception of milk. Without matter cognizable by the senses, there could be no awareness that there is milk. And without functioning taste buds, one could not taste milk and recognize its flavor as, for instance, sweet or sour.

Our human senses are limited to a certain range of materiality. Our eyes can detect wavelengths from 380 to 700 nanometers. Our ears can only hear frequencies from about 20 hertz to 20 kilohertz and lose sensitivity as we age. A sound that falls outside of this humanly audible range will not be perceived even though the sound wave hits our eardrums, and there will be no consciousness of this sound. And without recognizing an audible frequency as a sound, there can be no awareness of it.

The contact of the senses with the sense-objects produces feeling, which can be pleasant, unpleasant, or neutral. The perception of the object—that is, the cognizing of what is sensed through the sixfold base—along with the type of feeling that it produces leads to mental proliferation and sustained thought regarding the object.

Thus, the mentality factors (contact, feeling, perception, thought, and attention) and the materiality elements constitute the foundation for the establishment and operation of the sixfold sense base. This explains how the sixfold base arises dependent on mentality and materiality.

Meditation on the six senses fosters the cultivation, understanding, and appreciation of the necessity of the practice of sense restraint in the light of dependent origination. In *The Discourse on the Development of Faculties*, the Buddha asks the brahmin student Uttara how his teacher, the brahmin Parasariya, teaches his students the development of the faculties (*indriyas*).[28] The word *indriya* means chief of a particular function, and so each sense organ is the chief of the specific function it performs. The leading indriya is the mind, for it presides over all other functions. The term also refers to the spiritual faculties of faith, energy, mindfulness, concentration, and wisdom. However, in the context of dependent origination they correspond to the six sense faculties.

The cessation of the underlying tendencies arising from the six sense bases is called *salayatana nirodha*. It is the destruction, by means of the spiritual faculties, of the influxes of sensual pleasure, becoming, wrong view, and ignorance[29] that arise through the six senses. A common error is to think that spiritual progress is contingent on completely shutting out the senses, and this is precisely what the brahmin Parasariya was preaching. The Buddha immediately points out that if this were the case, then the blind would all have developed spiritual faculties—sensory deprivation isn't the way to liberation. He then delivers a profound teaching on what constitutes the supreme development of the faculties.

As soon as sense-contact arises, feeling arises. That feeling can be agreeable, disagreeable, or a mixture. From feeling, a whole gamut of unwholesome or wholesome states of mind can emerge. When paying full, undivided, mindful attention to feelings, one sees their arising, transforming, and fading away. One sees that they are conditioned, dependently arisen, and therefore impermanent. This leads to the understanding that these feelings are not worth holding on to, as they are like a flickering mirage in a desert. As a result, the mind turns to equanimity, which is sublime and peaceful. With sustained mindfulness practice, the establishment of equanimity becomes spontaneous. This discipline is the proper way to develop the spiritual faculties.

In his teaching on overcoming hindrances, the Buddha gives a simile of a drop of water in a hot iron pan. As soon as a drop of water falls into the pan it evaporates. Similarly, when paying mindful attention, unwholesome states that surreptitiously drop into the mind evaporate, and equanimity is restored.

CHAPTER 6

The Nutriment of Contact

J UST LIKE CONSCIOUSNESS, contact is a nonphysical nutriment; although the physical body touches something physically it is the mind that knows the touch through the nervous system. The basis of contact—the conjunction of sense, sense-object, and consciousness— occurs for each of the six senses: the eyes, sight, and eye-consciousness; the ears, sounds, and ear-consciousness; the nose, odors, and nose-consciousness; the tongue, tastes, and tongue-consciousness; the body, tangibles, and body-consciousness; and the mind, mind-objects, and mind-consciousness.

In social settings, eye contact is viewed as necessary for effective communication, and a lack of eye contact generally sends a wrong message to the listener and gives a very poor impression. This is one aspect of contact that is well understood in social interactions.

Another familiar form of contact is through touch. This is paramount for newborns; the touch contact of the mother allows the baby to develop. It is this contact that helps establish the bond between mother and child. When drinking the mother's milk, tenderly held in her bosom, the baby feels the mother's love. In turn, the mother feels the baby's love. And that relationship remains in the baby's mind for the rest of their life. So physical contact is indispensable.

Contact with nature and animals is also important and shows us how contact can generate feelings. Petting your cat or dog enhances its bond with you. And the quality of the contact determines the animal's response. If the contact is rough, the animal will be afraid or angry, which could cause all sorts of problems. Contact produces hormones that affect our health and state of mind, generating emotions according to the kind of contact that we experience.

Subsequently, we hold on to the feeling generated by contact, which can be pleasant, unpleasant, or neutral. The Buddha said that depending on the feeling, craving arises. Naturally, craving or clinging would arise if the feeling were pleasant. But what about when a rough, harsh, and unpleasant feeling arises? Would craving arise from a painful feeling? The answer is still yes; even troublesome feelings generate craving. When an unpleasant feeling arises, it is the craving to get rid of it that arises. And when a pleasant feeling arises, the craving to maintain it arises. So in both cases craving arises.

The arising of craving from contact involves thinking. Contact generates perception, recognition. When there is contact, we feel something and then recognize it. For instance, when we eat various kinds of food, we can distinguish one taste from another, even one sweet taste from another, such as an apple and a banana. Our taste buds can distinguish many different types of sweetness, and this recognition of the subtleties in sweet flavors begins with contact. Therefore, contact produces feeling, which generates perception. Perception in turn generates thoughts, which can be tainted by greed or inclined to letting go (renunciation), depending on the quality of the mind.

Contact itself is divided into two kinds: designation and impingement. Designation acts as an agent that brings to the mind the qualities of the object; contact with a sense-object occurs due to the presence of these qualities in the object. Anything that we perceive with the body is through recognizing the characteristic properties of objects. As discussed in chapter 4, the qualities of the material world around us can be classified in terms of the four elements. This group is called *form* or *materiality*. The qualities of the materiality group are hardness (earth), flowing or binding (water), heat (fire), and movement (air).

Impingement, meanwhile, is the direct contact of an object with the senses. Consciousness flows through the sense door where a stimulus occurs. So if the sense stimulus (the sense-object) is visual and the sense of sight is present, then consciousness arises. The meeting of the three is eye contact. However, in order to see the object, its characteristics have to be perceived through designation.

Therefore, without designation, impingement could not occur, for the six sense-consciousnesses need designation in order to arise. And obviously without impingement there would be no designation. The two are interconnected. This is why in *The Discourse on the Great Causation* the Buddha asked: "If the qualities, signs, themes, and indicators by which there is a description of a name group (mentality) were all absent, would designation contact with regards to the form group (materiality) be discerned?"[30] Without the mental factors (mentality group) there would be no discerning of the form in terms of its characteristics and hence no designation contact. Without the physical bodily senses, there could be no impingement contact.

Let us consider a concrete example. Suppose that you hear a squeaky screeching sound. The sound waves hit your functioning eardrum. Designation contact sends the message to your consciousness that there is this sound. Ear-consciousness arises. There is contact of the sound, your hearing, and your consciousness. Now you become aware of the sound and the quality of the sound. You have a label for it: squeaky. You don't like it. You have an unpleasant feeling. You start seeing in your imagination an image attached to the screeching sound, like nails on a blackboard. You develop an aversion to the sound, and mental proliferation occurs. You want it to stop. You crave its utter disappearance. You wonder who or what caused it. Furthermore, depending on craving, clinging arises. You get agitated; you want the noise to stop and begin to suffer. This clinging is desire. Contact is mental food. Your intense desire just gave you mental indigestion.

Impingement contact belongs to the mentality group: contact, feeling, perception, thoughts, and attention. Impingement—that is, direct contact—depends on consciousness, which depends on the mentality factors. Without the mental constituents, consciousness cannot arise. The mentality factors are connected to the materiality factors, and the flow of consciousness is through the six sense bases. Without the sense bases, the eye-, ear-, nose-, tongue-, body-, and mind-consciousness could not arise. Hence, the contact of the senses, sense-objects, and consciousness depends on the sense bases. Therefore, dependent on the sixfold base, contact arises, the fifth link of dependent origination.

CHAPTER 7

Feeling

FEELING REFERS to the physical and mental sensations that arise when the six senses contact the sense-objects. For most of our lives, from the day we come out of our mother's womb until death, as long as we are conscious, we feel. It is a ubiquitous mental sensation that arises dependent on contact, the sixth link of dependent origination.

Aside from being one of the mentality factors, it is also one of the aggregates, or "collections," because its various types belong to a collection of 108 categories. To begin with, there are six kinds of feeling that arise through our five physical senses and minds. Each of these six types can be pleasant, unpleasant, and neutral, giving us eighteen further types of feelings. These eighteen can arise regarding the past, present, or future, and each of these resulting fifty-four kinds of feelings can be with or without underlying tendencies of defilements (*asavas*). Hence, feelings are classified into a total of 108 categories.

For this last categorization, we remind the reader that asavas are residues that remain after the primary defilements have been overcome. All unenlightened beings have feelings with asavas. When these underlying tendencies are present in the mind, they inevitably yield thoughts of clinging. We cannot cling to anything unless the thought of clinging arises, and it will as long as asavas exist. Therefore, feeling that arises based on the existence of asavas is called *sasava*, or feeling "with asava," while feeling that arises without these underlying tendencies is called *niramisa* or *anasava*. A person who attains full enlightenment has feelings like anybody else, but his or her feelings arise without underlying tendencies and are therefore niramisa.

Feeling in any of these categories cannot exist by itself; it depends on the senses. For feeling to occur, sense, sense-object, consciousness, and contact must be present. Senses are the doors or conduits through which consciousness passes for sensations to occur. However, feelings cannot be categorized as perceivable merely through the sense doors. They are not directly seen, heard, touched, smelled, or tasted. Instead, feelings produce a mental response. They leave an impression, which is interpreted by the mind as pleasant or unpleasant. Neutral feelings are neither pleasant nor unpleasant and are generally unnoticed.

For instance, when going to a doctor we try to describe a pain that we may experience as throbbing, poking, piercing, and so on. But these words are just constructs to express feelings. We know that we are feeling something because of a response from our nervous system. Feelings that occur through the five physical sense-contacts are bodily sensations, while emotions are feelings that involve thinking and occur though mind contact.

As we stated previously, when a sensory object, sense, and consciousness come together, contact arises. And with contact, feeling arises. Feeling is not in the objects, the senses, consciousness, or contact, but only in their coming together. It is classified according to the sense organ based on which it arises. When a visual object comes into contact with the eyes, eye-consciousness arises, and so in this case feeling arises though the eye contact. Similarly, feeling arises through ear-, nose-, tongue-, body-, and mind-contact.

Feeling arises instantaneously and disappears just as quickly. And the object that led to the arising of a particular feeling must be reintroduced to the senses in order for this same kind of sensory feeling to be reproduced. The steps leading to the arising and disappearing of feeling happen so quickly that they appear indistinguishable. For example, when sound comes into contact with our ears, we are conscious of hearing that sound, and thus ear-consciousness arises. From this audible contact, feeling arises. Once the sound wave fades outside of the human audible range, the feeling that arose in dependence on contact resulting from the sound wave hitting our ear drums disappears. And an audible frequency must be reintroduced for the feeling of hearing to arise again.

It is important to understand that none of the sense organs by themselves have feeling, nor do contact or the consciousness pertaining to the senses. Feeling only occurs as a result of the conjunction of the four factors leading to its arising. The mind, mind-objects (thoughts), mind-consciousness, and mind-contact are also devoid of feelings. As for physical senses, feeling arises through the mind from the meeting of these four elements (sense-object, sense, consciousness, and contact).

A useful simile to understand the arising of feeling is that of a flute. The sound is not in the flute, just like feeling is not in the sense organ but depends on contact. Sound is produced by the propagation of vibrations in a medium (such as air) resulting from the displacement occurring between the molecules of the medium induced by a mechanical disturbance. This vibration involves compression waves that depend on the medium through which they propagate. So when we hear a flute being played, the sound depends on the vibration of the air molecules and the frequency of the combinations of holes being plugged. The holes themselves have no frequency. Feeling arises in the same way through the medium of the sense doors.

All sense perceptions have varying degrees of clarity and quality, depending on different internal and external factors resulting from the combination of the senses, sensory objects, and media. Feeling, for example, is a mind conditioner that arises through contact, and it leads to certain mental states as it is perceived as pleasant, unpleasant, or neither pleasant nor unpleasant. Pleasant sensations are agreeable, enjoyable, delightful, sweet—in other words, likable. They can be a pleasurable physical sensation or a joyous emotion. When a pleasant sensation occurs we generally cling to it because we like it very much and want it to last.

On the other hand an unpleasant feeling is painful, disagreeable, troublesome, sour—in other words, unlikable. It can be a painful physical sensation or a hurtful emotion. When an unpleasant feeling occurs we tend to reject it; we want to push it away. There is this constant tug-of-war between grasping what is pleasant and pushing away what is unpleasant. When the feeling is neither pleasant nor unpleasant it generally goes unnoticed, and so its underlying tendency is delusion or ignorance.

FEELING DOES NOT HAVE TO BE SUFFERING

Feelings are inevitable, but training the mind to deal with them is entirely up to us. *The Discourse to Nakulapita* recounts a beautiful story of an elderly, ailing gentleman named Nakulapita, who went to see the Buddha for council.[31] When in the Buddha's presence, he said, "I am now aged, come to the last stage of life. This body is often afflicted and ill. Let the Blessed One instruct me." The Buddha did not console Nakulapita but bluntly agreed with his own assessment of his worn-out physical condition. "It is so," said the Buddha, adding:

> If anyone carrying around this body of yours were to claim to
> be healthy even for a moment, that would be utter foolishness.
> But this is how you should train yourself. Tell yourself: even
> though I am afflicted in body, my mind will not be afflicted
> when painful feelings arise.[32]

The Buddha continued, saying that uncomfortable and painful feelings that arise are simply due to old age. His advice to Nakulapita is also applicable to our lives: when painful bodily feelings assail us, we should not let them affect our minds.

Elsewhere the Buddha elaborates on this point with the well-known simile of the dart.[33] Being hit by a dart represents physical painful feelings. But if one lets the mind be afflicted by the physical pain, it is like being shot with a second dart. When getting hit by a dart in life, don't let your mind get agitated. The pain arising from that dart will slowly fade away.

Nakulapita did not really understand the Buddha's instruction but felt too shy to press him further. He left the Buddha, feeling happy to have met the Master, but was still confused about the teachings. Fortunately on the way home he met the Venerable Sariputta, a chief disciple of the Buddha, who clarified the Buddha's teachings and dispelled Nakulapita's doubts. He explained how the decay and aging of the five aggregates lead to sorrow, lamentation, suffering, grief, and despair. Without mindfulness, this mental affliction invariably accompanies physical pain. Therefore, mindfulness of feeling (the second foundation of mindfulness practice) is of utmost importance to overcome mental suffering and avoid the second dart. We will discuss this practice in the following section.

Any feeling from any of the categories described in the previous section can be suffering, and while we cannot prevent a feeling from arising, we do not have to suffer from it. We have already discussed that when a pleasant feeling arises, it is only pleasant while it is present; when it disappears we experience displeasure. And when an unpleasant feeling is present we experience pain; when it disappears, we experience pleasure. When a neutral feeling is present, we don't notice it, although it also arises, transforms, and disappears, to be replaced with either a pleasant or unpleasant sensation.

Oftentimes, we romanticize feelings by glorifying a past event that we categorized as a wonderful experience. But feelings are always in the present moment. When we remember a joyous event, a pleasant feeling arises now. When we anticipate an enjoyable event, a delightful feeling arises in the present moment.

When a pleasant feeling arises we become attached to it; we like it, we delight in it. We want to maintain it, support it, and keep it forever. That unfortunately does not happen, because a pleasant feeling is impermanent like anything else. But we don't see this, and therefore we take delight in the pleasant feeling. We get carried away with it at the expense of everything else. This doesn't mean that we should not experience any pleasant feelings, but we should remember that a pleasant feeling—just like anything else—has a finite lifespan. Similarly, painful feelings do not last forever. No matter how painful a feeling is, there comes a time when it will subside and pass.

When a pleasant feeling arises, and while having a pleasant feeling, we have to deal with the underlying tendency to cling to it by adopting the following thinking process: "This is a beautiful and pleasant feeling. However, this will fade away. I should not be disappointed when it does fade away, because that is its nature." In the same way, when an unpleasant feeling arises we should not get too depressed or disappointed, because that unpleasant feeling is also impermanent. And when it does fade away, a more pleasant feeling will replace it.

Hence, to see feelings as they arise one must pay total, undivided attention to the present moment. When a pleasant feeling arises, we simply become aware of this particular feeling as a pleasant feeling. We must reiterate here the importance of not verbalizing when engaging in this practice. The mind must be so focused on observing the rise and fall of feelings that there is no room for verbalization. Similarly, when an unpleasant feeling arises we become aware of its arising. When a neutral feeling arises, one also becomes aware of it. No matter which one of these three categories a feeling falls into, we become mindful of it, watch its arising, its peaking, and its fading away.

The experience of pleasant and unpleasant feeling is clear: there is either pleasure or pain. But how do we know that there is a neutral feeling if it is not perceived? This is where confusion arises, for we are ignorant of neutral feelings. However, the existence of neutral feelings can be inferred. There is the beginning of a pleasant feeling and the end of that pleasant feeling, the beginning of an unpleasant feeling and the end of that unpleasant feeling, and again the beginning of another pleasant feeling and its end. We continuously experience the altering between pleasant and unpleasant feelings. However, there is a gap between the end of the pleasant feeling and the beginning of the unpleasant feeling and also between the end of an unpleasant feeling and the beginning of a pleasant feeling. A neutral feeling occurs in that gap. The beginning of a pleasant feeling implies that before it arose, there was no pleasant feeling. Similarly, the beginning of an unpleasant feeling indicates that before it manifested, there was no unpleasant feeling. Therefore, neutral feelings are in the gap between what is felt as pleasant and unpleasant.

The Buddha explains this with the simile of a deer hunter. After a while of hunting a deer, the hunter loses sight of it and only sees its footprints on the ground. At some point its trail seems to end at a large rock. The hunter circumambulates the rock and sees deer prints again. And thus, the hunter deduces that the deer had crossed over the rock. Similarly, when we see two feelings that appear one after another, there is a feeling between them, which we usually do not sense very strongly.

While pleasant and unpleasant feelings are strong and grab our attention, neutral feelings are much weaker and go unnoticed. It is only when we follow a pleasant feeling all the way from its rise to its cessation with total, undivided attention that we have sufficient clarity of mind to see the rise of a neutral feeling. With the cessation of that neutral feeling comes the arising of an unpleasant feeling. Similarly, it is only when we see the cessation of an unpleasant feeling with mindful attention that we can sense the presence of a neutral feeling.

Feelings arise, transform, and cease spontaneously. Therefore, in this mindfulness practice we do not try to control them. We just pay total attention to them and watch them come and go. We become aware of how sensations occur as a result of physical contact. For example, you feel warmth arising from touch or you experience a certain sensation or mental impression from the smell of soup cooking in the kitchen.

This practice applies to emotions as well. Emotions, which arise within the mind, have mental contact. At times we get lost in them; we call this being emotional. It is essential to learn to recognize an emotion as an emotion and to notice it as soon as it arises. We pay attention to it without any judgment, and let it go as it naturally fades away. By recognizing whenever a sensation arises and observing it changing and passing away, we develop the ability to observe the impermanence of feeling. Thus, one sees that with the cessation of contact, feeling ceases.

When the impermanence of feeling is not seen, one also does not see the perpetual change in the pleasantness of feelings. As a result the mind constantly oscillates between wanting and rejecting, greed and aversion, craving and loathing. This is how dependent on feeling, craving arises.

Overcoming our engrained negative tendencies entails hard work, going against the grain, against the current of our impulses. These deeply rooted negative tendencies are habits that result in unwholesome thoughts, words, and deeds. Some people are always angry, for example. Anger has become a habit for them, and their uncontrolled anger can and does often lead to embarrassment and all kinds of unpleasant consequences. This too is dependent origination. When anger arises, unpleasantness arises. However, anger can be overcome by mindfulness. But this requires effort in order to maintain our mindfulness at every moment, not to let it slip away. Sustained mindfulness is the way to overcome our tendencies to cling to what is pleasurable and reject what is unpleasant. If we do not cling to what is pleasant, then greed and the army of defilements that accompany it have no footing. If we have no aversion toward what is unpleasant, then hatred and its battalion of unwholesome servants are all defeated.

FEELING AS AN OBJECT OF MEDITATION

Feeling is used as an object of meditation in the second of the four foundations of mindfulness.

Even though feeling changes all the time, we can employ mindfulness to see how this occurs in detail during meditation. This practice is called mindfulness of feeling. Everyone knows what feeling is like, but knowing the process of its arising and dissolution requires a certain kind of effort, which involves paying undivided attention to feeling by employing mindfulness.

In the meditation on feeling—part of the four foundations of mindfulness—when one experiences a pleasant feeling, one knows that it is a pleasant feeling. *When* is a matter of time. Feeling arises at a certain point in time, and the mindful meditator understands that a particular feeling has arisen at that particular point in time and discerns its quality, whether pleasant, unpleasant, or neutral. Thus, the meditator sees the feeling and its inherent quality arising and passing away. When a pleasant or unpleasant feeling arises, at that very moment we become aware of that pleasant or unpleasant feeling. We would like to re-emphasize that paying total, mindful attention is absolutely necessary in order to know feeling in this way.

When a painful feeling arises we may be able to use a metric to describe its intensity. However, attachment to feeling will inevitably result in experiencing an increase in the pain-intensity scale. If we have no attachment to feeling, we will experience a painful feeling, but without suffering. Feeling by itself is not suffering; it is our mental state that creates suffering from feeling.

Hence, to avoid suffering one must understand feeling and how to handle it without attachment or rejection. This is achieved through meditating on feeling, a powerful object of meditation that can also lead to liberation. In this meditation, when a pleasant feeling arises one knows it is pleasant. But one does not verbalize the experience by saying to oneself, "Now I feel a pleasant feeling." The word *I* must be eliminated and the feeling must simply be felt, because *I*, *me*, and *mine* are the products of greed and ignorance. One just becomes fully aware of the feeling and its qualities exactly as they are and sees the feeling arising and passing away. In order to use the three kinds of feelings (pleasant, unpleasant, and neutral) as objects of meditation, mindfulness must be sharp, as neutral feelings are not easily discernible. In addition, discerning the underlying tendencies of greed, anger, and confusion that accompany pleasant, unpleasant, and neutral feelings is only possible when mindfulness is sharp.

It is essential to eliminate greed and ignorance from this practice and to become aware of the pleasantness of pleasant feelings when they arise—not before, and not after. At the very moment of its onset we must become aware of the pleasantness of a pleasant feeling. Similarly, when a painful feeling arises we must become aware of its unpleasantness without trying to escape or change it. One should not say, "I am in pain," but simply be mindful of the sensation of pain in the painful feeling.

When a neither-pleasant-nor-unpleasant feeling arises we must become mindful of that state, too. Most of the time, we are in a state of neither-pleasant-nor-unpleasant feeling. But since we are usually unmindful, this state is completely ignored. When a pleasant feeling arises, we must become aware of it and acknowledge it. When it fades away pain arises, and we must become mindful of that. And when pain disappears, again a neither-pleasant-nor-unpleasant feeling appears. Again we must become aware of it, and following its dissolution a pleasant feeling arises.

As discussed earlier, feeling can be with or without desire. When feeling without desire arises we must become mindful of the feeling and its qualities of both pleasantness and desirelessness. When a neither-pleasant-nor-unpleasant feeling arises without ignorance we must become mindful of it. This feeling is not nourished by ignorance but rather by wisdom, understanding, and letting go. When this feeling fades away, as per its nature, a painful feeling arises without anger or resentment.

In this practice one does not experience pleasure externally through the senses but internally through the mind. One experiences a deep state of peace and relaxation. This profound experience of peace, devoid of contact with external objects that cause the arising of greed, is very joyous and pleasurable. It spontaneously arises within us with the insight of the rise and fall of all phenomena. Since ignorance is not there to hide our view of the sequential and repetitive cycles of rising and falling, greed does not arise.

Normally ignorance blocks our clear view of impermanence so that when a pleasant experience occurs, greedy thoughts of holding on to this pleasantness invade our mind. Lacking mindfulness, we are generally unaware of the grasping tendency that assails our mind when a pleasant sensation is felt. As a result, pleasant sensations arise with greed. Lacking clear comprehension of impermanence, our mind becomes afflicted by its own greed. On the other hand, when we have knowledge and clear understanding of impermanence, we experience pleasantness without the underlying tendency of greed, and this leads to a profound state of inner peace.

Similarly, when we are mindful, ignorance does not interfere to confuse our mind when experiencing a neither-pleasant-nor-unpleasant feeling, because the rise and fall of all phenomena can be clearly seen. With this, there arises an equanimous feeling. We understand that the pain we are experiencing follows the dissolution of the neutral feeling that followed when the previously occurring pleasant feeling subsided. With this insight of the rise and fall of feelings, we develop a trust in the triple gem and in our own spiritual capability.

In *The Discourse on Right View* the Venerable Sariputta explains that understanding feeling is like understanding suffering. Using the scheme of the four noble truths, understanding feeling's origin is like understanding the origin of suffering, understanding its cessation is like understanding the cessation of suffering, and the path leading to its cessation is like the path leading to the cessation of suffering.[34] It is therefore essential to pay total, mindful attention to our feelings in order to understand how feeling arises and ceases. The way leading to the cessation of feeling is right understanding, but this doesn't require the annihilation of the senses. It simply necessitates understanding the process by which feeling arises.

With wisdom, one understands that the pleasure that arises from feeling depends on contact, and with the cessation of that same contact, the feeling that arose from it also disappears. Hence, one comprehends the danger in feelings that are inherently subject to change. Clinging to what is impermanent leads to suffering. Therefore, one gradually develops the wisdom to let go of feeling and of the attachment to pleasing sensations. This is how one escapes their lure.

CHAPTER 8

Craving

F OR AN IGNORANT person, the ubiquitous response to pleasant feelings is craving. Hence, craving arises dependent on feeling, the seventh link of dependent origination.

Craving is a mental state, a thought, a mental kamma, and therefore is one of the mentality factors. Everything we do pivots around craving because it is deeply entrenched in our minds and lives. Like a magnet with a powerful attractive force, it brings about rebirth when combined with ignorance, kamma, and consciousness. Craving, along with ignorance, is the link from one life to the next. But due to ignorance we do not see the danger in craving, which is why it has such a dominating and self-generating power. Even though craving is impermanent it repeats itself, along with delight and attachment. Its insatiability is such that it yields more craving, and as a result it leads to renewed existence in samsara.

There are three kinds of craving that we will explore: craving for sensual pleasures, craving for existence, and craving for nonexistence. Craving for sensual pleasures is the one that obsesses the mind the most. It involves desires connected with the five senses and the mind. Our entire life is dominated by wanting to see, hear, smell, taste, touch, and think about the objects of our desires. This craving is insatiable, and desire connected with sensual pleasures is endless because we always feel that there is something more to be experienced through the six senses.

The following simile illustrates this point. Imagine that a person owns a very large house. One fine morning he wakes up to find the house full of gold, miraculously poured in through every nook and cranny. There is so much gold that even his entire village could not use it all. Upon seeing this large fortune contained within the walls of his dwelling, he exclaims, "Gosh, I wish I had a bigger house!" That is the nature of craving. He does not think, "How could I share all this wealth? Why should I have so much gold?" Instead, he wants more.

But haven't we all experienced this? Overflowing shopping carts on Black Friday, mountainous servings of food at the all-you-can-eat buffet, the rush to fill whatever container we have whenever we get free stuff: these are all illustrations of what craving looks like. Day after day we have this endless and senseless urge to satisfy our senses. And it never stops. As soon as we are done satisfying one craving, another one pops up, and we chase after that one. And so we are never satisfied, never at peace. This brings much dissatisfaction, disappointment, sorrow, and suffering to our lives.

We attempt to satisfy our senses from the moment we are born until the time we die. But sometimes something is missing from our bucket list of sensual experiences. And thus we wish for another life to continue the chase after sensory satisfactions. Generally people reject the idea of death because they want to continue to exist. Even when thinking of the afterlife most people imagine that a form of their current personality will go on, and they wish to go on forever. It is the notion of I and the wish for its continuation that leads to craving for existence.

On the other hand, sometimes when people are depressed they wish to be annihilated, to disappear forever and cease existing. While craving for existence can sometimes lead to self-mortification in a misguided attempt to improve oneself, craving for annihilation generally causes self-indulgence. One prone to such a view would want to enjoy all the pleasures of the present life to the utmost, and often excessively so.

Craving for sensual pleasures is a deeply rooted mental state that is difficult to eliminate. As explained in chapter 1, this makes it a fetter. When learning about the challenges posed by the pull of the senses in the practice, one may wonder if the senses are fetters to the sense-objects or vice versa. It is precisely this question that the Venerable Kotthita asked the Buddha's chief disciple, the Venerable Sariputta, as related to us in *The Discourse to Kotthita*.[35] The Venerable Sariputta answered using a simile of a pair of black and white oxen joined with a yoke. He said that one could say neither that the white ox is the fetter of the black ox nor that the black ox is the fetter of the white ox. Rather, the fetter is the yoke that is joining them together, keeping them bound to one another, and not either one of them. In the same way, the eye is not a fetter to the eye-object, and it is desire and craving that arise from the two of them together that is the fetter. Thus desire and craving, which cause suffering, arise in dependence on both the eye and the eye-object.

Let us explain how this comes about. When the eye and the visible object come together, one may think, "I see the object." We insert the *I* between the eye and the form. Along with *I* there is desire, and it is this desire that binds the eye and the physical object. The binding factor is the fetter. The same can be said for the other four physical senses and the mind. Just like with the physical senses, it is desire and craving that bind the mind and thoughts together.

THE SIMILE OF THE SEAMSTRESS

Craving sews one life to another. It is like moisture that exhibits the property of adhesion and keeps us glued to the cycle of samsara. The following simile illustrates this particular feature of craving. One day, the story goes, the Buddha gave a profound and succinct sermon to a group of monks. He said only:

> Having understood both ends,
> the wise one does not stick in the middle.
> I call him a great man:
> he who has here transcended the seamstress.[36]

After uttering these words, he left without giving any further explanation. After lunch the monks assembled in the Sangha hall for the customary Dhamma discussion, and this time the topic was the Buddha's brief statement, with one monk asking: "What, friends, is the first side? What is the second side? What is in-between? And what is the seamstress?" Another monk said:

> Contact, friends, is the first side; the origination of contact is the second side, and the middle is the cessation of contact. The seamstress is craving, because craving is the cause of existence that joins the two ends together. The one who knows this directly for himself or herself and understands it with correct wisdom can make an end to suffering in this very life.

The practice of serenity and insight is the means to put an end to suffering. Serenity is *samatha*, which is attained through tranquility meditation, and insight is *vipassana*, seeing from the root. These should be known by direct experience and not indirectly through mere bookish knowledge. Teachers can only point the way and explain what serenity and insight are, but in the end one must directly know them from one's personal experience. With mindful reflection, we can see how the seamstress (desire), joins the ends (contact and the arising of contact) together while ignoring the middle (the cessation of contact). The seamstress binds both ends and forgets the middle, which causes craving and clinging.

The monk who led the discussion made another astute point: that craving is the cause of existence. Why is that? Repeated desire has delight and clinging, which is like glue. When the seamstress arises, ignorance arises as well and makes us forget the middle, cessation. Not seeing cessation, we are stuck in desire. Desire, as we have seen, is the cause of rebirth. And so the seamstress keeps us stuck in the rounds of becoming.

Then a second monk said that the past is one end, the future is the second end, and the present is the middle. Craving is the seamstress because she sews beings to the rounds of existence. The Buddha's advice is to forget the past, not to ponder over the future, and to keep the mind in the present with mindfulness, which allows keen observation of the rapid changes occurring in the present. But the seamstress, desire, holds on to the past, ponders over the future, and forgets about the present. That is the job of the seamstress, which is the nature of desire, the essence of clinging. It inhibits the clear and unobstructed view of what is happening now. We habitually remember and dwell on the past, recalling all sorts of sensory experiences. But actually, only the memory of the past—not the past itself—remains in the mind, and that too is changing and fleeting. We never fully recall events as they occurred because our memory of the facts falters, and our perception of what really happened is always somewhat distorted. Once we are done thinking of the past, we tend to immediately jump to the future. And all those future things, sights, sounds, smells, and tastes that we dream of? They too are impermanent. The remedy for this chronic compulsion of the mind to constantly oscillate between the past and the present is mindful meditation.

The ever-changing nature of mentality and materiality must therefore be understood with wisdom in order to keep the mind in the present moment and stop wasting precious mental energy over the mirage of the past and future. When we understand the nature of mentality and materiality, we know that all we've ever felt, seen, heard, smelled, touched, tasted, and thought about are gone. So we should keep looking at our minds mindfully in order to see what is happening now, at this very moment.

THE ORIGIN OF CRAVING

Dependent on feeling, craving arises. Feeling in turn arises through our senses. We feel while seeing, hearing, smelling, tasting, touching, and knowing mind-objects. It permeates our entire lives and is therefore a powerful factor. As long as feeling exists, craving arises. Craving involves both desire and clinging, and from desire, more desire arises.

To understand craving and to keenly observe its arising and passing, one must be aware of where it takes root. The Buddha said that whatever in the world has a pleasant and agreeable nature, it is there that craving arises when it arises, and it is there that it settles down when it settles down. To understand the meaning of this statement, let us first describe where craving arises. Our senses perceive what is agreeable. Since we have six senses (including the mind), craving arises through the six sense doors. The senses bring in pleasurable sensations. Hence, there is craving for seeing, hearing, smelling, tasting, touching, and thinking. This is craving for the senses themselves. But there are also the sense-objects consisting of forms that are pleasant and agreeable. Naturally, craving arises there too.

To be aware of a sensation, consciousness must be involved. Earlier, we explained that consciousness goes through the sense doors when there is a sensorial stimulus coming from a particular sense. Therefore, craving arises from eye-, ear-, nose-, tongue-, body-, and mind-consciousness. When the senses, sense-objects, and consciousness come together, contact arises. Hence, craving also arises from these six kinds of contact. Similarly, there are six kinds of perceptions connected with the senses. When what we perceive is agreeable and pleasant, craving for perception occurs.

When perception arises, we begin to think. Six kinds of volitional formations connected with sense-objects then occur. Mental proliferation takes place as craving begets craving due to the pleasant nature of the objects perceived and examined. The initial thought of the six sense-objects gives way to sustained thinking and repetitive contemplation. This repetition acts like a wheel spinning in the mud so that craving gets stuck or established in sixty different places, with ten possible phenomena for each of the six senses:

1. the sense itself;

2. the sense-object;

3. sense-consciousness;

4. contact resulting from the meeting of the sense, sense-object, and sense-consciousness;

5. feeling born of sense-contact;

6. perception of the sense-object;

7. volition regarding the sense-object;

8. craving for the sense-object;

9. the initial thought about the sense-object; and

10. sustained thought about the sense-object.

We constantly try to satisfy desire in this life. However, we are never fully satisfied, and thus we keep repeating the endless chase to fulfill our desires. This quest goes on day after day, month after month, and year after year. In fact, it consumes our entire lives. And whenever we ask ourselves the question "am I satisfied?" we always get the same answer: "not yet." There is always another desire that is not yet satisfied. With these unfulfilled desires in the mind, our lives come to an end at some point, and we die hoping to satisfy them in our next life. But there we find ourselves in the same predicament, as desire arises from the same sixty places.

Hence, there is seemingly no end to this. This is why the Buddha said that the beginning of desire is indiscernible. There is no point in time before which a state of desirelessness can be found. To make matters worse, the presence of ignorance in the mind blocks clear understanding. Therefore, when our mind is fettered by desires and our view is blocked by ignorance, the result is endless rounds of death and rebirth in samsara, which is represented as a cycle to stress the point that this process has no beginning and no end. This situation seems at first quite hopeless. However, the Buddha did find a way out, the method to end this cycle. That which can end samsara, this endless cycle of birth and death, is called the

Dhamma. And when the Buddha went to Benares to teach his first sermon, he started rolling the wheel of Dhamma to end it.

Even though the Dhamma cannot be seen with the eyes, it remains our escape hatch from suffering. In the same way, even though samsara is invisible to the eyes, the workings of the mind that trap us in it—jealousy, greed, craving, and suffering—can be directly experienced. All these factors are mental states that can be perceived not by the five physical senses but by the mind. So can we see the invisible Dhamma with the invisible mind? At this very moment, while reading these words, you can see your invisible mind and the invisible Dhamma. You can experience mental states arising from seeing the words on the page and from understanding or not understanding what you are reading. You are the only one who can see that. It is a personal experience of which you are the sole owner. You are the one who can see the Dhamma cycle happening in your own mind.

In *The Discourse on the Great Causation* the Buddha explains that in dependence upon feeling, there is craving. In dependence upon craving, there is pursuit. In dependence upon pursuit, there is gain. In dependence upon gain, there is decision-making. In dependence upon decision-making, there is desire and lust. In dependence upon desire and lust, there is attachment. In dependence upon attachment, there is possessiveness. In dependence upon possessiveness, there is stinginess. In dependence upon stinginess, there is safeguarding. Because of safeguarding, various evil, unwholesome phenomena originate. These unwholesome acts involve warfare, fighting, quarrels, slander, insulting speech, and lies.

Everything happens in your mind. When you talk, write, perform any deed whatsoever, watch your mind at all times in order to guard it against defilements and prevent craving from invading it. You should never put the blame on anyone else for your moods. You must not point a finger at others when things do not go according to your liking but rather at yourself. Look at your own mind to see the invisible greed, anger, jealousy, and all the other defilements that are the real cause of your suffering. Looking at the mind must be done objectively, without a sense of guilt or self-deprecation and without trying to uncover an external cause of depression or blaming others or your circumstances. Look at your mind. You created it. Thus, you are responsible for its moods. If you create a wholesome state of mind, you are responsible for this. Likewise, if you create an unwholesome state of mind, you are also responsible for the moods that such a mind brings.

Therefore, this invisible cycle is in you. And the way to end this cycle of birth and death is in your mind right now. If you end greed now, you attain liberation now. If you end greed one minute later, you attain liberation one minute later. If you end greed tomorrow, you attain liberation tomorrow. Henceforth, the end of this beginningless cycle of samsara is in sight. It is within our power, will, mindfulness, practice, determination, and commitment. When we make this kind of commitment, we can end this cycle whenever we choose to do so.

Craving brings sorrow and fear. As we have explained earlier, it is craving and ignorance that ensnare us in this cycle of repeated life and birth. This was the Buddha's insight that led him to discover dependent origination, which lays out the causes and conditions resulting in repeated rebirths. Therefore, when the Buddha attained enlightenment he declared, "the eye arose in me." This is the eye of wisdom that arose when he saw dependent origination, and with it he saw the beginning and end of craving and the cycle of samsara. Craving can be found in our very own mind. Understanding it is a personal exploration that must be undertaken individually, for the solution to abandon it is also in our own minds.

HOW TO ABANDON CRAVING

People sometimes say that they want to experiment with sensual pleasures: trying a particular kind of food or drink or indulging in a certain sensory experience. Before his enlightenment the Buddha experimented too. However, he had the insight to conclude that there would be no end to this exercise and that this type of behavior would keep him in bondage indefinitely. He understood that there is a great danger in sensual pleasures—not that they cause immediate harm or risk to one's life (although some sensory pleasures can definitely be lethal) but that sense enjoyments are impermanent. And because they are impermanent they can never be satisfactory.

And so, understanding this, the Buddha began searching for something else. His deep insight led him to the complete abandonment of sensual pleasures. This point must be properly understood: This abandonment is not the forceful shunning of pleasurable sensation as in sense mortification. Rather, it is the wisdom to see the danger and degradation in these pleasures.

When we acquire a possession with greed, we stingily hold on to it and go to great lengths to protect it, thereby accumulating much stress. Great disputes and wars have started in the name of material gain. Craving is the cause of many personal and social problems. Therefore, the solution to these problems is to remove craving, which is attained by abandoning our attachment to sensual pleasures. Note that the key word here is *attachment*. Letting go of attachment does not mean that we must torture ourselves and make abstractions of what is necessary to live a happy and healthy life. We must use our senses, but we must do so with wisdom, because with wisdom we understand how the influxes operate in us.

In chapter 1 we described the influxes of sensual pleasures, becoming, ignorance, and wrong views. To restrain these influxes, we have to adopt a certain code of conduct that involves four kinds of right effort. The first two involve preventing the unwholesome mental states of greed, hatred, and delusion from arising in our thoughts, words, and deeds and overcoming them when they do arise. When unwholesome thoughts form in your mind and harsh words are right on the tip of your tongue, you must put on the breaks and stop them right there and then. This doesn't happen automatically. It requires some effort. The general tendency of the mind is to cater to the lowest common denominator, using as an excuse the widely accepted, unwholesome behavior of others around us. In order to free ourselves from suffering, this tendency must be abandoned. When there are no unwholesome thoughts, we must make an effort to culti-vate wholesome ones, the third kind of right effort. This also demands a certain amount of mental exertion, going against the grain, swimming upstream. If we are not mindful, the current of human nature with all its defilements will inevitably carry us downstream. Once wholesome thoughts have entered the mind, we should practice the fourth kind of right effort by maintaining, sustaining, and nourishing them for as long as we can. The mind should always be ready to apply itself to these four right efforts necessary to restrain the influxes. And mindfulness is the tool we use to apply them.

Another essential practice concerning restraint is patience, which the Buddha called the highest austerity. Patience does not imply that we should be a mat for people to wipe their feet on; it isn't cowardice. Patience goes hand in hand with wisdom. When we speak, we speak with patience. This doesn't mean that we should remain quiet most of the time. It means waiting for the right time to speak, with the right attitude, with speech that is correct, precise, and to the point. In other words, patience supports effective speech.

The Buddha exemplified this with his actions. One time, when he was staying in Jeta's woods at Savatthi, a haughty brahmin arrived in the grove and started to verbally assault him for no good reason, hurl-ing insult after insult. The Buddha waited calmly until he had run out of words, and then asked him the following question: "Brahmin, do you have any friends and relatives?" "Of course," said the brahmin, "I have friends and relatives." The Buddha continued, "Do you visit them?" "Yes," said the brahmin. "Do you bring them any gifts when you visit them?" asked the Buddha. "I never go empty handed. I always bring them gifts when I visit them," he said. Then the Buddha asked a further question: "Suppose, brahmin, that they refused your gifts. What would you do in that case?" "Well, in that case, I would take the gifts home and enjoy them myself," replied the brahmin. "Likewise, brahmin, you have given me a gift that I do not accept. Please take it home to enjoy it for yourself," said the Buddha.[37]

Patience is in the mind, and so is impatience. It is our response to external triggers. But we do not have to accept unwholesome gifts and thereby lose our mental serenity. Of course, when we feel that our buttons are getting pushed, this is easier said than done. However, patience can be cultivated. It comes with wisdom. With wisdom, forbearance and tolerance develop so that we can tolerate anything that life may throw at us with calmness and equanimity, and as a result we can think, speak, and act skillfully in accordance with the Dhamma.

The Venerable Sariputta was often praised by the Buddha for his forbearance. It was in reference to an assault the Venerable Sariputta endured while going on his alms round one day that the Buddha spoke the following verse recorded in the *Dhammapada*:

One should not strike a brahmin
And a brahmin should not set [anger] loose.
Shame on one who hits a brahmin
And greater shame on one who sets [anger] loose.[38]

One day, the story goes, a brahmin wanting to impress his followers decided to provoke the Venerable Sariputta. While the monk was mindfully walking to the village to collect alms, the brahmin snuck up behind him and hit him violently in the back. But the Venerable Sariputta did not even look back to see his assailant. Shocked by the composure of the Venerable monk, the brahmin felt deep pangs of remorse and got on his knees to beg for forgiveness, which the Venerable Sariputta fully granted.

In chapter 1 we presented the six methods to overcome influxes: seeing, restraining, using, avoiding, removing, and developing. While these methods are auxiliary aids, mindfulness is the key to attain liberation from suffering and supports these methods all on its own. Mindfulness has become a cliché, but it must be properly understood for one to avoid practicing it the wrong way. And what is the difference between right and wrong mindfulness? When planning an unwholesome deed, the mind can be focused and concentrated in order to achieve the goal at hand, but this is still wrong mindfulness. Right mindfulness, on the other hand, is always wholesome and beneficial.

If you have practiced mindfulness your entire life, constantly thinking about its practice, focusing on the breath at every moment, and have not reduced greed by one iota, then you have been wasting your time and practicing wrong mindfulness. But if your mindfulness leads to reducing your greed, hatred, and delusion, it is right mindfulness, and every minute of this practice is beneficial. Think of the practice of right mindfulness as an investment account. Every moment of this practice goes into that account and adds up to your attainment and movement toward liberation. Practicing right mindfulness does not mean that you have to sit in one place all day long. It can be practiced anytime, anywhere. Anytime greed arises, one becomes aware of it and lets it go. Whenever one does this, the mindfulness account increases.

Ideally mindfulness is present all the time, whether we sit with our eyes closed in meditation or are fully involved in activities. Right mindfulness is therefore a constant practice, a personal attainment that has nothing to do with mere theory. This repeated practice makes mindfulness strong and so powerful that one day one is able to overcome greed, hatred, and delusion. The practice is gradually developed to achieve this goal. Of course this does not happen suddenly but bit by bit, moment by moment.

The objects of mindfulness can be anything that exists and that we experience in our lives. These objects all have clear and unmistakable marks: impermanence, unsatisfactoriness, and nonself. To see these marks you must look at the world differently and look at objects from the root. This is not so easy when the senses are constantly bombarded by sensory impressions. That is why we practice by closing our eyes in meditation and withdrawing our senses from external impressions.

The methods that we have described so far are means for overcoming craving. It is not always present; it arises and passes away depending on the situation. When whatever conditions responsible for the arising of craving pass, so too does craving. Consider the following analogy laid out by the Buddha. Suppose there were a great tree with all its roots going downward and across. That tree would be sustained and well nourished by its sap, and it would stand for a long time. In the same way, sense gratification, born out of ignorance, keeps us in a state of suffering, going endlessly through the cycle of birth and death. Now, suppose that someone cut the tree down at the base and put the trunk back in place so that the tree would look whole once more: that tree would still never grow again. Cutting down the tree can be likened to the destruction of craving. This reflection on the arising and ceasing of craving is of the utmost importance to help us understand craving and so put an end to it.

CHAPTER 9

Clinging

CRAVING, if left to run amok, leads to clinging, the eighth link of dependent origination. Clinging arises when the mind holds on to our body, feelings, perception, thoughts, and consciousness. As explained in chapter 1, these are called the five aggregates of clinging, and consequently of suffering. Just like craving, clinging is a thought, a mental construct. Thoughts of clinging keep us captive, bound to the five aggregates. While imprisoned by the aggregates of clinging, one is far from liberation and experiences disappointment, stress, despair, and all sorts of tensions—in short, suffering. Even a thought of clinging to the five aggregates of suffering is suffering!

As taught by the Venerable Sariputta in *The Discourse on Right View*, clinging is related to the four noble truths of suffering.[39] Clinging is suffering. Therefore, the origin of suffering is the origin of clinging, the cessation of suffering is the cessation of clinging, and the way leading to the cessation of suffering is the same path leading to the cessation of clinging. After explaining this, Venerable Sariputta addressed the question of the origin of suffering, which is clinging. And the cause of clinging is craving. Thus, with the cessation of craving, clinging ceases. And when clinging ceases, suffering ceases.

Clinging arises from a sequence of dependently arisen mental phenomena. Let us briefly review these steps: When the senses come into contact with sense-objects, consciousness arises. When the senses, sense-object, and consciousness come together, contact arises. As a result of this contact feeling arises. Feelings depend on our mental state; objects by themselves do not have pleasantness or unpleasantness. It is the mind that labels them as pleasant or unpleasant. If the object is pleasant, a mental state of craving develops. The wish to sense, again and again, the same object that led to a pleasant feeling ensues. This pattern, reinforced by desire and strengthened by repetition, results in clinging. All these states arise in the mind and cease in the mind. Therefore we have to look into the mind to find the secret of happiness. The solution to our suffering is not somewhere outside of ourselves but in our own mind.

So let us investigate in detail how clinging happens. The Venerable Sariputta explained that there are four kinds of clinging: clinging to sensual pleasures, to views, to rites and rituals, and to doctrines of self. In chapter 1 we discussed these fetters in more detail, explaining their gradual destruction at the different stages of enlightenment and that they are obstacles on the way to being liberated from suffering. The kind of clinging that usually dominates the mind is clinging to sensual pleasures. For example, objects are presented to your eyes. Now you see the words on the page of this book. As soon as your eyes meet the printed words, consciousness arises. Due to the immeasurably fast rise of consciousness, as soon as your eyes meet the visual objects, contact arises. All the steps involved in contact—opening the eyes, seeing, and recognizing the object—are mental activities.

The next mental activity is feeling. Although it is sensed somewhere in the body, feeling requires consciousness. If consciousness does not arise, there can be no feeling. As explained in chapter 7, feeling is something not physical but mental. As soon as feeling arises, a sensation is perceived as either pleasant, unpleasant, or neutral. And the pleasantness, unpleasantness, or neutrality of the feeling is solely based on our state of mind, because objects by themselves do not have these characteristics. It is the mind that labels objects as pleasant, unpleasant, or neutral and gives value to them. In fact what one person likes may be quite disagreeable to another. Therefore feeling is an individual and personal mental state over which we have no control. What we can, however, control is how we react to feelings.

If the object is pleasant, another mental state develops: desire, which intensifies into craving. The craving to sense the same object of desire again and again comes from the mind's conditioning. The mind has been trained through repetition to pursue the object of its desire by indulging the senses to contact and delight in that same object. Note that appreciation for the object is also a mental state.

The next mental state that arises, following the repetitive indulging in objects of craving, is clinging. Desire is reinforced when the same mental state that craves a pleasurable object becomes habitual. A desire that is thus reinforced becomes very powerful. As a result the mind is as if glued to the object of desire. The longer we pay attention to the object and dwell on it, the stronger our desire and the more tenacious our clinging to it. We cling to sights, sounds, odors, tastes, tangibles, and thoughts—in short, to the world of the six senses. It is as if a world connected to the senses emerges whenever they become active. For instance, when we see something, the world of sight is born. Depending on the quality of the mind, worlds of thoughts arise and uncountable images are formed in the mind.

In every moment, we are born into the visual, auditory, olfactory, gustatory, tactile, and mental worlds. Immersed in these worlds, we cling to the objects they contain. When their content depletes, we miss what we held on to and suffer. These worlds appear and disappear from moment to moment. We cling to them because we are unable to see their perpetual appearance and disappearance due to ignorance. When one sees dependent origination—when this arises, this arises; when this passes away, this passes away—one understands that there really isn't anything to hold on to.

Clinging arises in the mind when we do not see the underlying mechanics of what is happening. In fact we do not actually cling to the object but to the thought of the object that arises in our mind, and thus we obsess about it. However, if we were to see the entire mechanism that leads to clinging, we would understand that there really isn't anything to cling to. But due to ignorance and craving, we fail to see this entire process. Ignorance is so strong that it distorts our senses and convinces us that what we crave will remain and bring us comfort and solace. Seeing with right understanding the mechanism of sensual thoughts arising in the mind, craving cannot arise.

Once we understand with proper wisdom that all that has come to be in the realm of the six senses is subject to passing away, we are able to let go of our grasp on these worlds. Having let go, we soar above lamentation, grief, and sadness to a world of perfect equanimity beyond all suffering.

Living in the World Without Clinging

Whenever the topic of nonclinging is discussed, the role of desires for the pursuit of activities and occupations necessary to daily life usually comes up. This argument comes from a confusion about the difference between interest and clinging. Of course one must have a desire or interest in pursuing the various activities necessary for our continued existence in the world, but this does not require clinging. The following simile illustrates this point.

Our ancient Buddhist texts tell a story of a legendary war between the devas (deities) and asuras (demons). The asuras lost the war, and Sakka, the king of the devas, ordered his attendant to bind the asura king, Vepacitti. So Vepacitti was bound in five places—his hands, legs, and neck tied by a heavy chain—and dragged to the heavenly realm. But Sakka offered him a deal to regain his freedom: if Vepacitti admitted that the devas were right and the asuras were wrong, he would immediately be freed from his shackles and allowed to stay in the deva realm to enjoy heavenly bliss. Now Vepacitti found himself in quite a predicament. How could he betray his asura people by saying that they were wrong? On the other hand, if he were to go along with Sakka's request he could enjoy the pleasures of the heavenly realm. But Vepacitti's pride kept him from surrendering. In either case, he was bound. His predicament is a riddle illustrating that as long as one is bound by fivefold sensual pleasures, there is no end to suffering.

The Buddha explains that greed is just like this. When one is enmeshed in ignorance, it is impossible to live without greed; and at the same time, greed brings about much suffering. Vepacitti represents the gamut of negative traits headed by greed, while Sakka embodies all the good qualities developed by mindfulness. When both sides are in a tug of war, mindfulness intervenes, serving as judge and justice. It is the balancing act that allows us to regain restraint in order to bring greed back under control. Without mindfulness we remain like Vepacitti, shackled by the cords of sensual pleasures, bound by greed.

Human nature has always struggled with the idea of abandoning what is pleasant, and even some disciples of the Buddha rebelled against foregoing sensual pleasures. In *The Discourse on the Simile of the Quail*, the Venerable Udayin tells the Buddha how much suffering has been averted by restraint and abandonment.[40] But some monastics seem to have rebelled against the rules of restraint laid out by the Buddha. When told, "Abandon this," they would disregard the Buddha, obstinately thinking, "What a mere trifle. Our teacher is too demanding!" As a result, the small thing to be abandoned became a big, strong, thick yoke.

To illustrate the danger, drawback, and painful consequences of clinging to what is pleasant, the Buddha tells the Venerable Udayin the story of a captive quail that is unable to unbind itself. The quail is bound up by a rotting creeper. But since the quail is a feeble creature, she is unable to free herself. Even though the creeper is rotting, to the quail it appears very strong and solid. In the same way, the little things and habits pertaining to the pleasures of the senses, which at first seem so insignificant and benign, become very big fetters when one is unable to abandon them. The Buddha further explains that when one is able to overcome clinging, all fetters connected with greed become like a weak and rotting creeper. For a royal tusker elephant that is tethered, a simple twist of his body would be enough to free him from a strong fetter, which to him is no more than a mere weak and rotting creeper.

A serene and peaceful life free from clinging is like a hang glider gracefully flying on the horizon, while clinging makes the glider of serenity crash. Learning to fly a hang glider provides a direct simile for how grasping works and how letting go sets one free. One grasps the bars due to fear borne out of a sense of self or me. The orientation and balance of the wings together with the position of the glider's nose is what controls its flow through air currents. As soon as one clings to the bars they become off balance and the nose tilts downward. When one grasps, the mind is absorbed in holding on tightly, paying no attention to the position of the glider's nose. When one does not see things as they are, heedfulness is gone due to fear. One trains to barely touch the down bars at lift off, controlling the glider by the slightest push. With time and effort this becomes natural, and one can easily take off and stay in the air some two hundred feet or more, gently controlling the apparatus with the down bar. The pilot's success rests in his or her ability to overcome grasping. This little victory over oneself gives a great sense of freedom as one glides through the air. So, if flying in a mundane way can give one such a thrill, can you imagine the joy of soaring to the heights of spiritual liberation?

CHAPTER 10

Becoming

WHAT WE BECOME tomorrow, the day after tomorrow, or in the next life depends on the current state of our mind. What we constantly ponder shapes the characteristics of our mind. The purity of our mind governs the kind of thoughts we have, which dictate our choices. And our choices in turn yield our future.

Becoming can be an upward or downward movement leading to a life of improvement or degradation. We carry wholesome and unwholesome seeds in our minds. Consider the seed of anger, for instance. What if, instead of watering this seed by plotting ways to express this anger at the slightest vexation, we decided to practice patience? To assist us in this practice, we might recall all the problems and embarrassments that come from letting anger run amok. Seeing this outcome in the lives of others and ourselves, we would be inclined to cultivate the mind to develop patience. In the course of time, by sustaining mental discipline, we would become a patient person.

When one listens to and practices the Dhamma, an inner transformation occurs that brings about a wholesome state of mind and a happy life. Having used the Dhamma as a raft to cross the river of samsara, one lets go of it, too. For it is through not clinging to anything at all that one is fully liberated. When clinging ceases, becoming ceases.

This isn't easy. Great religious wars have been fought over clinging to doctrines, with each religion maintaining that followers of other creeds have wrong view. But wrong view is not the belief in a particular deity or ritual but rather looking at, or conceiving, something in an erroneous way. In other words, it is believing that something false is true. At its most fundamental level, wrong view is vehemently holding on to the view that what is impermanent is permanent, what is impure is pure, and what is nonself is self. Hence, led by desires and clinging, we go on becoming.

The belief in permanence is deeply engrained in the human mind. It clings to the belief of eternal love, perpetual heavenly experience, being forever young, although the idea of a forever-hell hardly seems appealing. This clinging leads the mind to conjure all kinds of castles in the air, dreams, and future projections. Growing up we are encouraged to have big dreams for our future: becoming a doctor, a lawyer, a philosopher, or anything that sounds prestigious enough. Having plans for a profession in accord with one's skills and natural abilities is not the problem, but getting caught in a web of desires will inevitably result in remaining bound in samsara, where we will continue to satisfy more desires. This is how becoming arises dependent on clinging, the ninth link of dependent origination.

The three types of craving for sensual pleasures, existence, and non-existence constitute the moisture in the field of kamma that leads to the corresponding types of becoming: renewed sensual becoming, becoming with form, and formless becoming. The domain in which kamma ripens produces the corresponding type of becoming: kamma ripening in the sensual domain gives rise to sensual becoming, and so on. Depending on kamma, one can take rebirth in the form or formless realm, meaning that one can take rebirth with or without form.

Interestingly enough, *becoming* means changing. While becoming is the result of clinging, which is due to not seeing impermanence, the truth of impermanence is right there in the word *becoming*. But what if we did see impermanence, the rise and fall of all conditioned things, and were able to let go and thus overcome clinging? The mind would remain anchored in the present moment. All pondering over the future and holding on to wishes and hopes would be gone. There would just be the total freedom of being in the present moment, and no more becoming.

 *Birth*

I N THE PREVIOUS chapter we described how becoming is the result of clinging, our desires and attachments, which carry over in this life and the next. According to Buddhist teachings, birth is the precipitation into the womb, generation, manifestation of the aggregates, and development of the sixfold sense base (the basis for contact). This is how a being arises.

With the arising of being comes the arising of birth. With the cessation of being comes the cessation of birth. The way leading to the cessation of birth is the noble eightfold path of right view, intention, speech, action, livelihood, effort, mindfulness, and concentration. We will discuss how the noble eightfold path leads to the cessation of birth and all the troubles that birth entails in more detail at the end of this book.

According to the formula of dependent origination, three things come together at the moment of birth: the mother's egg, the father's sperm, and a being. The Pali term for this being is *gandhabba*, which signifies that which is ready to move. The root word *gandha* means "going," and therefore *gandhabba* means a being that is ready to go. The gandhabba is not a mature being with fully developed feelings, perceptions, and thoughts that is waiting around, looking for the place of rebirth that meets the conditions of their choice. If this were the case, no one would choose unpleasant surroundings to take rebirth; everyone would choose the most pleasant environmental and living conditions.

However, there is no time to select a place. At the moment of death a powerful energy containing the seed of consciousness instantaneously transfers to a new life according to the person's kamma; and from there it begins to grow. When a person dies their consciousness becomes the seed; kamma, the field; and craving, the moisture for rebirth to occur. The transition between death and rebirth occurs immediately, without an in-between resting place. Consciousness changes extremely rapidly and reappears as a different consciousness when birth occurs. This is the power of consciousness combined with kamma and desire.

Let us now describe how consciousness comes into play at the time of death and the process by which it flows from life to life. There are four factors present at the last moment of life: kamma, the sign of kamma, the place of rebirth, and the sign of the place of rebirth. At the time of death, we see the different kinds of kamma—wholesome, unwholesome, and imperturbable—that we have committed throughout our lives. An ignorant person has only a partial understanding of the unwholesome, the wholesome, and their roots. As a result, this person would be subject to rebirth even though they may have done a great many good deeds during their lifetime. A mental image of the sensory perception that was predominant at the time of committing the kamma is presented to the mind; this is called the sign of kamma. For instance, it could be an instrument in the case of a musician. Similarly, a dying person perceives a sign characterizing the place of rebirth.

Consciousness is present in each of these four factors, and it must be for volitional activity to take place. Volitional formations (sankharas) arise with consciousness and are born out of ignorance and greed. Fueled by these formations, consciousness moves from one moment of consciousness to the next by a process of cloning. At each moment, consciousness creates an instance of itself before fading away. This clone is the next moment of consciousness, which possesses the characteristics of the previous instance of consciousness. Similarly, to a child inheriting genes from his or her parents, the cloned instance of consciousness inherits the characteristics of the parents' moment of consciousness.

While the clone inherits the tendencies of the moment of consciousness that gave rise to it, it is not the same consciousness but rather another moment in consciousness with characteristics inherited from the previous one. This is why consciousness changes from one moment to the next. However, if consciousness is free from sankharas, as in the case of an arahant, the cloning process does not occur in the absence of craving, because there is nothing to power it. Thus, there is no relinking of consciousness to a new existence. During rebirth the cloning process is powered by craving for existence. And so, when the last moment of consciousness ends in one life, the next moment of consciousness arises in the next one.

During fecundation the first moment of consciousness takes root. Life begins not when the sperm and ovum join but when this so-called gandhabba appears and joins them. When these three combine birth takes place and life begins. It is at that time that the seed of consciousness takes root, and once this seed is planted the mother begins her work. She is the support structure feeding this embryo. Within twenty-four hours of fertilization the fertilized egg begins dividing into many cells through mitosis. As the cells divide, they acquire characteristics that dictate their properties. The cells develop into the blastocyst, which is composed of layers that evolve into the various components of the embryo. By the eighth week the embryo develops into a fetus, and the brain develops during the fetal stage of pregnancy. The baby comes out crying, which activates the lungs. From that time on the baby's physiology takes on the responsibility for the body's development.

Rebirth will necessarily occur whenever there is desire, which is intrinsically linked to kamma. This is so because desire, or its culmination in craving, leads to actions in thought, speech, or deed that produce kamma. Kamma in turn produces the conditions for becoming, and becoming leads to birth. Hence, depending on becoming, there is birth, the tenth link of dependent origination.

REBIRTH AND KAMMA

The topic of rebirth is often highly contested. Since most of us cannot remember our past lives this is hardly surprising. However, whether one believes in rebirth or not the fructification of evil kamma can hardly be denied if one is observant. If one lives skillfully one is well accepted and respected by society, while unskillful actions are blamed and censured by the world at large. This is how one's deeds yield results in the present life. But if the slate is not wiped clean at the time of death, then surely the actions performed in this life condition the next.

In *The Discourse to the Kalamas*, the Buddha explains that even if there were no rebirth, harmful deeds such as taking a life would yield painful consequences in our current existence.[41] On the other hand, if there were rebirth, then suffering would follow us in this life and the next. Similarly, wholesome deeds yield happiness in both this life and the next. So, whether one believes in rebirth or not, in the end what really matters is the skill with which we live our life.

But even though we can't recall our previous births, let us assume that there is rebirth. We've ascertained that the pleasant or unpleasant conditions of our next life are determined by our actions in this life. What about our tendencies and natural abilities? Let us consider the case of a teacher who loved his job. According to the Buddhist teachings, at the moment of death certain images (called *kamma nimitta*) connected with his role as a teacher would form in his mind. He might see a school, a classroom full of children, or a blackboard. This image would be most pleasing to him, and this pleasing thought would propel him to take rebirth under conditions favorable for him to become a teacher again. The way we live our life conditions our last thought, which sets the stage for our next birth.

This point is beautifully illustrated in *The Discourse to the Dog-Duty Ascetic*.[42] In the town of Haliddavasana in the Koliyan country, there lived a dog-duty ascetic called Seniya, who lived like a dog, while his friend Punna was an ox-duty ascetic who lived like an ox. One day these two friends went to see the Buddha. After paying his respects, Punna said that his friend's austere practice was to eat only food thrown on the ground. He wanted to know what Seniya's destination would be in his next life, but the Buddha told him not to ask this question. Undeterred, Punna repeated his question a second and a third time.

Since the Buddha could not dissuade him he gave the following answer: Because Seniya had developed the habits and behavior of a dog, his mind had become dog-like. As a result, he would take rebirth as a dog. Seniya's belief that his asceticism would lead him to become a god constituted wrong view, the consequence of which was rebirth in a woeful plane or the animal realm. When he heard this prediction, Seniya, the naked dog ascetic, wept.

And then Seniya inquired about the fate of Punna, who had also behaved his whole life like an animal. He as well was heading for rebirth in the animal realm, and he too felt sorrowful. Their tears were not so much for the sorrowful prospect of their next lives but more for having wasted so much time following the wrong path and not having heard the Dhamma sooner.

The Buddha, out of compassion for them, taught them about dark and bright kamma, the ripening of dark and bright kamma, and about kamma leading to the destruction of kamma. This kamma that leads to the ending of kamma, the Buddha taught them, is neither dark nor bright, and so too is its ripening. Performing kamma to end kamma is neither good nor bad kamma and is performed by using mindful reflection in order to eliminate greed, hatred, and delusion as soon as they arise. This relates to chapter 2, in which we explained that any action committed intentionally with a mind gripped by greed, hatred, and delusion is kamma. Therefore, destroying greed, hatred, and delusion leads to the annihilation of kamma. In order to do so, one must follow the noble eightfold path and fully understand dependent origination in descending order, beginning with the cessation of ignorance and culminating in the destruction of suffering, to be discussed in more detail later.

Having thus understood the Dhamma, the naked dog- and ox-duty ascetics went forth in the monastic order of the Buddha, and shortly thereafter they both joined the ranks of the arahants. This story illustrates that our behavior in this life determines the outcome of our next life. While this outcome is governed by the way we have lived our lives up to the present, our next choices in line with the Dhamma can alter it for the better. An observant practitioner would notice that even within a single day, their actions at one moment have repercussions in the next. Therefore, it is only logical that this flow of cause and effect would not stop at the end of this life but carry on to another.

CHAPTER 12

Death and the Arising of
This Entire Mass of Suffering

THE ELEVENTH LINK of dependent origination is the irrefutable fact of life that most people want to avoid thinking about: dependent on birth, death. Birth inevitably culminates in death, the twelfth step of dependent origination. However, reflecting on death is of great benefit. Suppose you found out that today is your last day to live and that you know of a practice that can give you a good rebirth or, better yet, enlightenment. Surely you would exert every effort and focus all your attention on this practice during the last few hours that you have in this life. To reflect on death is to recall the impermanence of life and awaken the spiritual urgency to liberate the mind from influxes by the practice of sustained mindfulness.

In *The Discourse on Mindfulness of Death*, several monks gave the details of their practice on this topic.[43] One monk said that if he lived only a night and a day, he could accomplish much to achieve liberation. The length of time given grew shorter and shorter, until the last two monks said that if they could only live long enough to chew their food or breath in and out, then they could accomplish much. Only the remarks of the last two monks were deemed heedful by the Buddha, for they understood that mindfulness must be sustained at every moment, with every breath, and they developed mindfulness of death acutely for the sake of ending influxes:

> Mindfulness of death, when developed and pursued, is of great fruit and great benefit. It gains a footing in the deathless, has the deathless as its final end. Therefore, you should develop mindfulness of death.

This practice requires anchoring the mind in the present moment and mindfully observing whatever arises in us. This necessitates heedfulness and constant effort. While we generally tend to think that the messengers of death are always at someone else's door, we must remember that we can die at any age. We have a tremendous opportunity to liberate ourselves from suffering in this very life, and we should not let this chance pass us by.

Through right effort one can overcome desire and lust; with the complete destruction of craving the mind is liberated. When craving is destroyed one attains enlightenment and the darkness of ignorance is forever gone. But while in the darkness of ignorance, by practicing mindful reflection we can put an end to the endless samsaric cycle. And it can start right now by paying total, undivided attention to what is happening within us at this very moment. In *The Discourse on a Single Excellent Night*, the Buddha stresses the unpredictability of death and the importance of this very moment:

> Let not a person revive the past
> Or on the future build his hopes;
> For the past has been left behind
> And the future has not been reached.
> Instead with insight let him see
> Each presently arisen state;
> Let him know that and be sure of it,
> Invincibly, unshakeably.
> Today the effort must be made;
> Tomorrow Death may come, who knows?

No bargain with Mortality
Can keep him and his hordes away,
But one who dwells thus ardently,
Relentlessly, by day, by night—
It is he, the Peaceful Sage has said,
Who has had a single excellent night.[44]

Now let us review the links of dependent origination and see how they culminate in sorrow, loss, and despair—this entire mass of suffering that the Dhamma can bring to an end. With ignorance as a condition, sankharas arise. Consciousness arises dependent on sankharas, and with the establishment of consciousness, mentality and materiality come to grow. With mentality and materiality as a condition, the six-sense basis arises. Depending on the six-sense basis, contact arises. With contact as a condition, feeling arises, which can be pleasant and agreeable. Sense gratification causes craving, and craving leads to clinging. Clinging gives rise to becoming. And becoming results in birth.

As soon as birth occurs, the process of aging starts. Along with aging comes decrepitude: bones break, hair grows gray, skin wrinkles, our life force declines, and our mental faculties weaken. Youth disappears, and we lose those who are dear to us. Along with loss comes grief, sorrow, despair, and lamentation, this entire mass of suffering. Whatever is pleasant today will be gone tomorrow. Such is the nature of all conditioned things. The more one grasps and clings to what is dear, the more one suffers and the longer one remains in samsara.

Reflecting on Impermanence

OUR FIVE AGGREGATES perpetually arise and pass away with tremendous speed. Today's scientific advancement allows us to understand the actual physical process involved in sensorial perception. The transmission of sensory information occurs when activated neurons send out electrical impulses, each of which occurs at a rate of approximately 150 meters per second. A neuron is activated as a result of pressure, heat, light, or adjacent neurons. If the stimulus is above the neural threshold, a change in the neuron electrical potential occurs. The potential difference alters the neuron membrane permeability that produces an ion current that runs along the membrane and triggers a neighboring neuron. After transmission, each neuron returns to its resting potential. Each neural activity is a sequence of arising transmissions through electrical or chemical activity and a subsequent cessation of that same activity from one neuron to the next. There are approximately 86 billion neurons in the human brain, a comparable order of magnitude to the number of stars in the Milky Way. Each neuron can have up to fifteen thousand connections with other neurons through synapses.[45] These data provide some scientific backdrop for us to get some insight into the rapidity of the rise and fall of neural activity—in a word, impermanence.

It is precisely impermanence that the Buddha wanted us to see. While having a scientific understanding satisfies the mind and assists us in clarifying the concept of impermanence, actually seeing impermanence implies paying total, mindful attention to one's experience in the present moment. This reflection yields profound benefits for the practitioner. In *The Discourse on the Perception of Impermanence*, the Buddha uses ten similes to explain how, when cultivated and developed, the perception of impermanence is a supreme practice that effectively exhausts sensual lust, the desire for form and formless existence, ignorance, and the conceit "I am."

> It eliminates all sensual lust, all lust for existence, all ignorance; it completely uproots the conceit "I am" just as a ploughman cuts through buried roots . . . a reed-cutter cuts down reeds . . . and a bunch of mangoes are cut off at the stalk. Just as a roof peak is the chief of rafters . . . the kalanusari is the most fragrant root . . . the red sandalwood is the most fragrant heartwood . . . the jasmine is the most fragrant flower . . . the wheel-turner is foremost among princes . . . the moonlight outshines all the stars . . . and the blazing sun in the autumn Indian sky dispels darkness, it eliminates all sensual lust, all lust for existence, all ignorance; it completely uproots the conceit "I am."[46]

By being fully diligent and heedful in contemplating impermanence in all formations, one can experience life and death at every moment.

Reversing the Chain

IN ASCENDING ORDER, the twelve steps of dependent origination present a sequence of causal dependence beginning with ignorance and culminating in the arising of rebirth. But in descending order, they present the sequential fall of each step, culminating with the total destruction of the root cause of our suffering, ignorance. In *The Discourse on Right View*, dependent origination is presented in the same way as the four noble truths, considering the origin of each step, its cessation, and the way leading to its cessation. The Venerable Sariputta asks for each step: What is it? What is its origin? What is its cessation? What is the way leading to its cessation?[47] The second question corresponds to the ascending order of dependent origination, the third to the descending order.

The cessation of each step from death to ignorance follows a causal relationship that is clearly observable by everyone. For all of us life culminates in death. Aging is a natural process that no one can escape. It starts with birth, and the endless cycle of death resulting from birth can only be broken with its cessation. Birth, the arising of a being with the manifestation of aggregates and the sixfold sense base, ceases when becoming ends. Becoming is the renewal of existence on the sensual, form, and formless planes resulting from clinging. Clinging is the moisture in the field of kamma that leads to becoming. Once it terminates, so does becoming. When craving for forms, sights, sounds, smells, tastes, tactile objects, and ideas ceases, clinging ceases. When feelings born of eye-, ear-, nose-, tongue-, body-, and mind-contact cease, craving for these same six sense-objects also ceases. When contact (that is, the meeting of the six senses, the sense-object, and sense-consciousness) ends, so does the feeling that arose from that contact. When the six sense bases (the eye-, ear-, nose-, tongue-, body-, and mind-base) cease, contact ends. The mentality factors (contact, feelings, perception, volition, attention) together with consciousness and the materiality elements of air, fire, water, and earth give rise to the sixfold base. Hence, with the cessation of mentality-materiality comes the cessation of the sixfold base. When consciousness arises, contact, feelings, perception, volition, and attention arise, and when consciousness ceases, these mentality and materiality factors cease. Consciousness arises based on volitional formations through the six senses. Thoughts and consciousness always arise together. When volitional formations cease, consciousness ceases. All three kinds of volitional formations—bodily, verbal, and mental—end with the cessation of ignorance. Ignorance in turn is the lack of knowledge regarding the origin, the cessation, and the path leading to the cessation of aging, decay, despair, lamentation, and suffering.

And what is the way leading to the cessation of suffering resulting from birth, death, becoming, clinging, craving, feeling, contact, the sixfold base, mentality and materiality, consciousness, volitional formations, and ignorance? It is the noble eightfold path, the first step of which is right understanding, the proper understanding of impermanence, unsatisfactoriness, and nonself. Everything that is impermanent is unsatisfactory and nonself. This includes all the elements of dependent origination, for whatever arises passes away. Volitional formations arise and pass away. They do not remain in the mind. When we understand that volitional formations arise and pass away together with consciousness, we have right understanding. This insight is the first step of the noble eightfold path.

Based on this, right intention arises. It too arises and passes away, together with consciousness. Right speech, right action, right livelihood—all arise and pass away along with volition and consciousness. At every moment volition and consciousness arise together and pass away together. Every effort is made with volition. Along with volition, consciousness arises. Every moment of mindfulness arises with volition and consciousness, and when volition passes away, so does consciousness. When we practice the noble eightfold path, we clearly see arising and falling from one moment to the next. We understand that once consciousness has arisen and fallen, it will arise and fall again not as the same consciousness, but as a new instance of consciousness. Similarly, when volition arises and falls it arises again as a new one. Volitional formations recondition the already conditioned body, feelings, perceptions, thoughts, and consciousness and in turn cause more volitional formations, which can be wholesome, unwholesome, or imperturbable. This applies to kamma as well: any act by body, speech, or mind done with volition produces kamma, which can likewise be wholesome, unwholesome, or imperturbable.

To fully appreciate the importance of following the eightfold path, let's return to these three kinds of kammas, discussed in chapter 2, and the types of actions that lead to their specific results. Wholesome, or punna, kammas are bright and lead to positive outcomes, which encourage us to perform more wholesome kamma. The outcome of such punna kamma has repercussions in this and future lives. To illustrate how potent punna kamma is, it is said that the earth, Mount Meru, and the ocean would all come to an end before meritorious kammas would be exhausted. Hence, wholesome kammas could never bring about the end of samsara. And since remaining in samsara amounts to suffering, such kammas do not lead to liberation from suffering.

At first glance, this seems contradictory. On one hand it is necessary to perform what is wholesome and sustain the desire to perpetuate these bright kammas in order to yield positive outcomes; on the other hand this perpetuates our existence in samsara. Unwholesome (dark) and wholesome (bright) kammas breed dark and bright kammas, respectively. But the kamma that either leads to the destruction of kamma or is based on the volition to abandon the kind of kamma that is unwholesome with dark results, wholesome with bright results, or a mix of unwholesome and wholesome with dark-and-bright results is called a kamma that is neither dark nor bright with neither-dark-nor-bright results. And it is this kamma that leads to the destruction of kamma. For example, the seven enlightenment factors discussed in chapter 1—mindfulness, discrimination of phenomena, energy, joy, tranquility, concentration, and equanimity—are practiced for the purpose of letting go of greed, hatred, and delusion. As a result, they constitute a kamma that is neither dark nor bright with neither-dark-nor-bright results, and they lead to the destruction of kamma.

Abandoning the desire to commit kamma leads to the destruction of the influxes of sense pleasures, becoming, ignorance, and wrong views. This renunciation starts with right understanding. In other words, following the noble eightfold path—right understanding, intention, speech, action, livelihood, effort, mindfulness, and concentration—is kamma that leads to the destruction of kamma.

Right understanding is knowing that all conditioned things—the wholesome, the unwholesome, and the imperturbable—are impermanent. Just as the sun sheds its light on every object, so too must our awareness of impermanence shine on everything we experience through our mind-body complex. Not seeing impermanence in all conditioned things is ignorance. One must abandon ignorance and arouse true knowledge, which is the complete understanding of impermanence, unsatisfactoriness, and nonself. It is the knowledge of suffering, the cause of suffering, the end of suffering, and the path leading to the end of suffering. With the fading away of ignorance and the arising of true knowledge, one would not generate any volitional formations of any kind. Not generating any volitional formations, one would not cling to anything at all. Not clinging to anything, one would not be shaken. Not being shaken, one would personally attain nibbana. And having put an end to ignorance, one would thus come to the realization that birth is destroyed.[48]

Dependent origination presents a roadmap for the arising of the causes and conditions that lead to suffering and their cessation. Rather than a dry theory, it is a self-exploration of the dependent arising and ceasing of

our aggregates that leads to the insight to see things as they are: impermanent, unsatisfactory, and nonself. Seeing this with deep insight is the key
to liberation from suffering. This is the way to end kamma, becoming,
birth, death, sorrow, lamentation, pain, grief, and despair.

Acknowledgments

WE THANK RICHARD ZEIKOWITZ for his meticulous proofreading of the manuscript. We are grateful to Michael Butcher, editorial associate at Wisdom Publications, for his exceptional attention to detail and diligence in fine-tuning this manuscript.

Abbreviations for Pali Canon Citations

AN	Anguttara Nikaya
Dhp	Dhammapada
DhpA	Dhammapada-atthakatha
DN	Digha Nikaya
MN	Majjhima Nikaya
SN	Samyutta Nikaya
Sn	Suttanipata

Notes

1. SN 12.1–2.
2. Ibid.
3. Nyanaponika 2008, 2.
4. DhpA III 417–21.
5. SN 12.2; Bodhi 2000, 534–36.
6. The Pali word for greed is *tanha*, which means "moisture." When you plant a seed, it will not grow without moisture. You have to water it. And when you have dry cement, it won't bind together until you pour water onto it.
7. MN 22.
8. AN 6.44.
9. SN 22.89.
10. Dhp 153–54; Fronsdal 2005, 40–41.
11. A celibate life dedicated to spiritual practice.
12. Sn 2.4.
13. SN 22.72.
14. Sn 3.12.
15. SN 22.79.
16. MN 18.
17. DhP 1–2; Fronsdal 2005, 1.
18. MN 136.
19. MN 136; Ñāṇamoli and Bodhi 1995, 1058–59.
20. SN 42.8.
21. Dhp 116–22; Fronsdal 2005, 31–2.
22. The Buddha's cousin Devadatta developed evil wishes toward the Buddha and grew deeply jealous of his fame. And so he devised a plot to kill him by pushing a big rock from a hilltop just as the Buddha was walking by. The plot failed— the rock hit an obstacle on its downward course and shattered. But a splinter from the rock injured the Buddha's foot.
23. MN 18; Ñāṇamoli and Bodhi 1995, 203.
24. MN 38.
25. MN 43; Ñāṇamoli and Bodhi 1995, 387–95.
26. SN 12.12.
27. Dhp 237–38; Fronsdal 2005, 62.

28. MN 152.
29. In Pali these are *kamasava, bhavasava, ditthasava,* and *avijjasava.*
30. DN 15.
31. Nakulapita means "father of Nakula." Nakula was fairly famous, and as a result the villagers named him after his son.
32. SN 22.1.
33. SN 36.6.
34. MN 9.
35. SN 35.191.
36. AN 6.61; Bodhi 2012, 950–53.
37. SN 7.2.
38. DhP 389; Fronsdal 2005, 100.
39. MN 9.
40. MN 66.
41. AN 3.65.
42. MN 57.
43. AN 6.19.
44. MN 131; Ñāṇamoli and Bodhi 1995, 1039.
45. Brotherson 2009.
46. SN 22.102.
47. MN 9.
48. MN 140.

Bibliography

Bodhi, Bhikkhu, trans. 2000. *The Connected Discourses of the Buddha: A Translation of the Saṃyutta Nikāya*. Boston: Wisdom Publications.

———. 2012. *The Numerical Discourses of the Buddha: A Translation of the Aṅguttara Nikāya*. Boston: Wisdom Publications.

———. 2017. *The Suttanipāta: An Ancient Collection of the Buddha's Discourses Together with Its Commentaries*. Boston: Wisdom Publications.

Brotherson, S. 2009. "Understanding Brain Development in Young Children, FS-609" *Bright Beginnings* 4: 1–8.

Buddhagosa. 1970. *The Commentary on the Dhammapada*. Vol. 3. Edited by H. C. Norman. London: Luzac & Company, Ltd.

Fronsdal, Gil, trans. 2005. *The Dhammapada: A New Translation of the Buddhist Classic with Annotations*. Boston & London: Shambhala Publications.

Ñāṇamoli, Bhikkhu, and Bhikkhu Bodhi, trans. 1995. *The Middle Length Discourses of the Buddha*. Boston: Wisdom Publications.

Thera, Nyanaponika. 2008. *The Roots of Good and Evil: Buddhist Texts Translated from the Pali with Comments and Introduction*. Kandy, Sri Lanka: Buddhist Publication Society.

Walshe, Maurice, trans. 1987. *The Long Discourses of the Buddha: A Translation of the Dīgha Nikāya*. Boston: Wisdom Publications.

Index

A

aging, 25, 93, 131, 135
analogies/examples
  concert, 40
  for craving, 101–2, 103–5
  dart, 92–93
  deer hunter, 95
  for feeling, 90, 91
  fermentation, 16
  Grand Canyon, 11
  house and house-builder, 28
  for kamma, 137–38
  king punishing bandit, 73
  for mindfulness, 35, 83
  mirage/illusion, 39, 71
  for nonclinging, 119–20
  for perceiving impermanence, 134
  for perception, 86, 87
  poisonous snake, 15
  raft, 15–16, 121
  soiled cloth, 26–27
  tree, 114
  for volitional formations, 51–52
Ananda, 23–24
anger, 3–4, 17, 18, 24–25, 33–34, 54–55, 62, 67, 96, 108, 112, 121. *See also* hatred
arahantship, 12, 27, 33, 36, 125, 127
ascetic practices, 14, 126–28

B

becoming, 17, 32, 74, 121–22, 135
birth, 4, 11, 28, 109, 123–28, 129, 131, 135, 138. *See also* rebirth
body (physical), 3–4, 20, 25, 28, 31, 37–38, 42, 46, 48–49, 50, 51, 75, 81, 85, 86, 92, 116. *See also* materiality
brahmacharya life, 31
breath, 8–9, 46, 129
Buddha
  enlightenment of, 1, 4–6
  stories of, 14, 74, 87, 92, 103–4, 107–8, 109–10, 111–12, 119, 127, 145n22
  See also Pali suttas

C

clinging, 74, 115–18, 135
  and becoming, 121, 122
  and ignorance, 27, 37
  and suffering, 100
conceit (*mana*), 17, 25–26, 41–43, 134–35
concentration, 9, 23, 30, 33, 36, 51, 82, 138
conditioned phenomena, 2, 45–46, 47, 49–50, 74, 83, 122, 131, 137, 138
  three characteristics of, 10–11, 17, 34
consciousness, 41, 56–57, 69–73, 136
  and birth, 124–25
  and contact, 87
  nutriment of, 73–75
  and rebirth, 75–76
  and sixfold base, 81
  and volitional formations, 137
  See also gandhabba; mind
contact, 70, 74, 75, 78, 81, 85–88, 136
  and craving, 104
  and feeling, 90–91, 99–100
craving (*tanha*), 12, 13, 28, 41–43, 74, 75, 135

abandoning, 109–14
and birth, 125
and clinging, 117
and consciousness, 75
and contact, 86, 87, 104
origin of, 105–9
three kinds of, 101–3
three types of, 122
and volitional formations, 49–50
See also desire; greed

D
death, 5, 59, 76, 102, 129–31, 135
dependent origination, 1–2, 9, 115–16,
  127, 131
  reversing, 135–39
  twelve links of, 3–6
  See also individual links
desire, 12, 18, 40–41, 101
  and clinging, 117
  and craving, 103
  and ignorance, 5–6, 107
  and rebirth, 104–5
  removing, 33
  for sensual pleasure, 17, 23–24
  See also craving (*tanha*); greed; lust;
    volitional formations (*sankhara*)
Devadatta, 145n22
Dhamma, 15–16, 107–8, 121
  clinging to, 15–16, 23
  investigation of, 35
Dhammapada, 27–28, 112
  on kamma, 60–61
  on rebirth, 76
  on thoughts, 55
*Discourse on a Single Excellent Night,
  The*, 130–31
Discourse on Being Devoured, The, 49
Discourse on Khemaka, The, 26
Discourse on Mindfulness of Death, The,
  129–30
Discourse on Right View, The, 99,
  115–16, 135
*Discourse on the Destruction of Craving,
  The*, 70–71

*Discourse on the Development of the
  Faculties, The*, 82
Discourse on the Great Causation, The,
  87, 108
*Discourse on the Great Exposition of
  Kamma, The*, 58
*Discourse on the Greater Set of Ques-
  tions and Answers, The*, 72
Discourse on the Honeyball, The, 69
Discourse on the Horn Blower, The,
  58–59
*Discourse on the Perception of Imperma-
  nence, The*, 133–34
*Discourse on the Simile of the Quail,
  The*, 119
*Discourse on the Supreme Blessings,
  The*, 32
Discourse to Kotthita, The, 102
Discourse to Nakulapita, The, 92
Discourse to Suradha, The, 42
Discourse to the Dog-Duty Ascetic, The,
  126–28
Discourse to the Kalamas, The, 126
dopamine (neurotransmitter), 31–32
doubt, 5, 18, 19, 20–22, 25

E
enlightenment, 130. *See also* liberation;
  "once-returning" (*sakadagami*)
equanimity, 33, 36, 74, 83, 112, 118, 138
eternalism, 12, 14–15, 29, 37, 122. *See
  also* permanence
ethics. *See* morality

F
faith, 22, 35, 82
fear, 25, 52
  of annihilation, 20
  and clinging, 120
  and craving, 109
feeling, 38–39, 46, 74, 82, 83, 89–92,
  135
  and clinging, 116–17
  and consciousness, 72
  and craving, 105–8
  as object of meditation, 96–100

and suffering, 92–96
and volitional formations, 50–51
fetters, 13, 102–3, 116, 119–20
  supporting ignorance, 18–19
  ten, 19–28
  See also individual fetters
five aggregates, 2–3, 8, 20, 26, 50
  of clinging/suffering, 37–41, 75, 115
  conditioning of, 46
  and volitional formations, 51–52
  See also mind-body complex; *individual aggregates*
food, 30, 31, 40, 57, 66, 75, 86, 109
form. *See* body (physical)
four noble truths, 7, 9, 11, 99, 115, 135

G
gandhabba, 123
greed, 11–12, 23, 25, 32, 33–34, 54, 57,
  67, 99, 119
  and ignorance, 13
  See also craving (*tanha*); desire

H
happiness, 10, 15, 36, 53, 55, 60, 62, 116,
  126
hatred, 1, 17, 19, 20, 24–25, 52, 53, 54,
  56, 62, 65, 67–68, 110, 127. *See also*
  anger
hindrances. *See* fetters

I
ignorance, 1, 7, 9–10, 27–28, 32, 47,
  99, 136
  cause of, 16–19
  and clinging, 27, 37, 118
  and desire, 5–6, 107
  destruction of, 4
  of extremes, 11–16
  of feeling, 39
  and sankharas, 45
  and volitional formations, 57
  See also influxes (*asava*)
illusions, 39, 71
impermanence, 6, 9, 20, 26, 29–30, 34,
  43, 133–34

influxes (*asava*), 16–18, 110–11
  destruction of, 83, 138
  overcoming, 28–33, 112–13
insight (*vipassana*), 3, 9, 12, 24, 104,
  130, 136, 139
  Buddha's, 109–10
  into impermanence, 27, 29–30, 33, 34,
  36, 75, 98–99
investigation, 33
  of Dhamma, 35–36
  objects of, 34, 37

J
Jain tradition, 59
jhanas, 53, 64–65
joy, 30, 33, 35–36, 52, 138

K
kamma
  and birth, 124, 125–28
  and death, 76
  ending, 138–39
  four categories of, 62–65
  mental, 101
  three kinds of, 137–38
  and volitional formations, 55–61
  wholesome *vs.* unwholesome, 65–68
killing, 56, 59, 63, 65, 67
knowledge, 7, 64, 104, 138
  of form, 46, 72
  of impermanence, 99

L
laypeople
  attaining enlightenment, 23–24
  overcoming influxes, 30
liberation, 9, 16, 33, 43, 51, 97, 109, 112,
  113, 120
  obstacles to, 19–28
  from suffering, 4–5, 12, 15, 36, 59, 137,
  139
  See also enlightenment
loving friendliness (*metta*), 25, 47–48,
  51, 53, 55, 59, 68
lust, 17, 47–48, 108, 130, 134. *See also*
  desire

M

Mara, 5–6

materiality, 46, 77, 78–79, 82, 86, 87, 136
  and consciousness, 72–73
  See also body (physical); nama-rupa; sense faculties (*indriyas*)

meditation, 8–9, 75, 113
  on feelings, 96–100
  hindrances to, 18–19
  metta, 47–48
  on six senses, 82–83
  See also insight (*vipassana*); jhanas; serenity (*samatha*)

memory, 18, 105

mentality, 46, 77, 78, 79, 82, 87, 101, 136
  and consciousness, 72–73
  See also nama-rupa

metta. *See* loving friendliness (*metta*)

middle way, 3, 16

Milayandaka, 23–24

mind, 55, 82, 110–11, 117
  and becoming, 121
  main functions of, 71–72
  and suffering, 108–9
  See also consciousness; mind-body complex; thoughts

mind-body complex, 2, 34, 37, 41, 45, 46, 73, 138
  See also body (physical); consciousness; five aggregates; mind

mindfulness, 30, 34–35, 104, 112–13, 136–37
  of death, 129–30
  of feeling, 93–100
  of unwholesome states, 83

monastic traditions, 8, 20, 30–31, 66, 127

morality, 20–21, 30. *See also* ten meritorious deeds

N

nama-rupa, 77–79. *See also* materiality; mentality

names. *See* mentality; nama-rupa

neural activity, 18, 31–32, 51–52, 133

nihilism, 14

noble beings. *See* arahantship

noble eightfold path, 3, 7, 23, 31, 123, 136–37, 138. *See also individual branches*

nonclinging, 118–20, 138

nonself, 9, 10, 20, 34, 113, 122, 136, 138, 139

nutriment (*ahara*)
  of consciousness, 73–75
  of contact, 85–88
  of feelings, 53

O

"once-returning" (*sakadagami*), 23–24

ordinary beings, 12–13, 45

P

Pali suttas, 8–9, 20, 21, 23–24, 26, 32, 42, 49, 58–59, 70–71, 74, 77–78, 82, 87, 92, 99, 102, 108, 115–16, 118–19, 126–28, 129–31, 133–34, 135. *See also individual discourses*

patience, 111–12, 121

peace, 2, 3, 9, 36, 52, 55, 83, 98–99, 120

perception, 39–40, 81–82, 133
  and consciousness, 72
  and contact, 86
  and volitional formations, 49–51

permanence, 10, 29, 122. *See also* eternalism

personality view, 20, 25–27, 29–30, 42–43, 102
  and desire, 103
  See also pride

pride, 5, 31, 37–38, 41, 119

R

rebirth, 14–15, 27–28, 74, 75–76
  and kamma, 62–63, 125–28
  in other realms, 64–65
  See also birth

restlessness, 18, 19, 25, 27, 36

right effort, 30, 32, 33, 35, 110–11, 130
right understanding, 11, 15, 17–18, 23, 33, 54, 68, 99, 118, 136, 138
rituals, 19, 22–23, 116, 121–22

S

samsara, 4, 11, 12, 15, 16–17, 19, 28, 40, 41, 107–8, 109, 121, 137
and craving/clinging, 101, 103, 122
and kamma, 62–63, 67–68, 71
and mind, 109
science, 133
self, view of. See personality view
self-indulgence, 12, 13, 14, 102
sense faculties (indriyas), 18, 68, 73–74, 79, 82–83
and contact, 85
and craving/clinging, 106–7, 117, 118
and feeling, 89, 90, 135–36
restraining, 8, 30
See also sixfold base
sense pleasures, 5, 6, 12–14, 19, 21, 23–24, 33, 53–54, 101, 102, 109–10, 116, 119
sense-objects, 49–50, 71, 78, 81, 82, 85–88, 89–91, 102–3, 106–7, 115–16, 135
sensory deprivation, 83
sensual misconduct, 59, 66
serenity (samatha), 2, 104, 112, 120. See also tranquility
seven factors of enlightenment, 27, 33–36, 138. See also individual factors
sixfold base, 81–83, 135–36. See also sense faculties (indriyas); sense-objects
sleepiness, 18, 19, 69
speech, 54, 70, 78
wholesome/right, 68, 136
wrong, 67
spiritual faculties, 82–83. See also individual faculties
stealing, 17, 59, 65–66, 67
stress, 10, 11, 17, 50, 52, 74, 110, 115

suffering (dukkha), 1, 2–3, 28, 74, 131, 138–39
cause of, 11–16
cessation of, 136
and clinging, 100, 115
liberation from, 4
and mind, 108–9
Suttanipata, 42

T

ten meritorious deeds, 48, 64–65, 67–68
thoughts, 19, 45–47, 50–55, 67–68, 86, 89, 91
of clinging, 115, 117–18
and kamma, 56–57, 61, 62–63
unwholesome, 33, 48, 59, 96, 99, 103, 110–11
See also mentality; volitional formations (sankhara)
three characteristics of existence, 10, 34–35
tranquility, 33, 36, 104, 138. See also serenity (samatha)
traumatic experiences, 18–19

U

underlying tendencies (anusaya)
cessation of, 82–83
of defilements, 89–90
and feeling, 89–90
of ignorance, 17–18, 38–39, 92
and kamma, 65
of personality view, 26–27
and sankharas, 45, 48, 55–57
and sixfold base, 82
unsatisfactoriness, 9, 11, 34, 113, 136, 138, 139
unwholesome states. See fetters

V

Venerable Sariputta, 72, 93, 99, 103, 112, 115–16, 135
virtual reality, 39

volitional formations (*sankhara*), 37,
  40–41, 45–46, 50–55, 124, 136–37
  as camouflage, 47–49
  and consciousness, 71–72
  and kamma, 55–68
  See also desire; thoughts

W
wisdom, 3, 7, 10, 16, 22, 30, 35–36,
  42, 43, 47, 54–55, 65, 82, 99–100,
  109, 110, 111–12. *See also* Dhamma;
  knowledge

wrong views (*ditthi*), 15–17, 20–21,
  28–29, 32, 42–43, 67, 68, 70, 110,
  121–22, 127, 138. *See also* personality
  view

About the Authors

BHANTE GUNARATANA was ordained at the age of twelve as a Buddhist monk in Sri Lanka, earned his PhD in philosophy from American University, and has led meditation retreats, taught Buddhism, and lectured widely throughout the United States, Canada, Europe, and Australia. Bhante Henepola Gunaratana is the president of the Bhavana Society in High View, West Virginia, where he lives.

VERONIQUE ZIEGLER earned her doctorate degree in experimental high-energy physics from the University of Iowa working on the BaBar experiment at SLAC National Laboratory in Menlo Park, California. She then took a research assistant position at the same lab and later a staff scientist position at Jefferson National Laboratory in Newport News, Virginia, where she currently works full time and is involved in the lab particle spectroscopy experimental program. In 2018, she started attending Bhante Gunaratana's Dhamma classes. She has been an avid Dhamma student ever since.

What to Read Next by Bhante G
from Wisdom Publications

Mindfulness in Plain English
20th Anniversary Edition

"A classic—one of the very best English sources for authoritative explanations of mindfulness."
—Daniel Goleman, author of *Emotional Intelligence*

Eight Mindful Steps to Happiness
Walking the Buddha's Path

"An astoundingly clear and joyful guide to living life at the deepest level."
—*Inquiring Mind*

Beyond Mindfulness in Plain English
An Introductory Guide to Deeper States of Meditation

"Bhante Gunaratana has done it again! There is practical logic and an almost startling common sense to the explanations that lead the reader smoothly through the various stages of meditative concentration."
—Ajahn Amaro, abbot of Abhayagiri Monastery

The Four Foundations of Mindfulness in Plain English

"The Four Foundations come to life. Drink long, drink deeply."
—Jon Kabat-Zinn

The Mindfulness in Plain English Journal

A mindful journal for a balanced life—based on the worldwide bestseller *Mindfulness in Plain English*.

Loving-Kindness in Plain English
The Practice of Metta

"*Loving-Kindness in Plain English* is a book that will bring more love into your life."
—Tara Brach, PhD, author of *Radical Acceptance* and *True Refuge*

Start Here, Start Now
A Short Guide to Mindfulness Meditation

"A timeless, clear, and beautiful introduction."
—Tamara Levitt, Head of Mindfulness at Calm

Buddhist Suttas for Recitation
With Bhikkhu Bodhi
A Companion for Walking the Buddha's Path

This unique volume includes carefully chosen discourses of the Buddha from the Pali Canon—presented in inspiring and accessible English with accompanying Pali—that convey the essence of the Dhamma.

What, Why, How

"This book can be of help to anyone's spiritual journey and meditation practice."
—Sharon Salzberg, author of *Lovingkindness* and *Real Happiness*

Impermanence in Plain English

With Julia Harris

"This simple yet deep guide points newcomers to insight meditation right to the heart of insight knowledge, and it encourages seasoned meditators to trust the joyful unfolding of this path of peace."

—Shaila Catherine, author of *Beyond Distraction*

About Wisdom Publications

Wisdom Publications is the leading publisher of classic and contemporary Buddhist books and practical works on mindfulness. To learn more about us or to explore our other books, please visit our website at wisdomexperience.org or contact us at the address below.

Wisdom Publications
132 Perry Street
New York, NY 10014 USA

We are a 501(c)(3) organization, and donations in support of our mission are tax deductible.

Wisdom Publications is affiliated with the Foundation for the Preservation of the Mahayana Tradition (FPMT).